The Moments When I Met God

Live manifestations of god which enriched my life

notionpress.com

The Moments When I Met God

Live manifestations of god which enriched my life

Jagadeesh Pillai

notionpress.com

Notion Press

Old No. 38, New No. 6

McNichols Road, Chetpet

Chennai - 600 031

First Published by Notion Press 2016

ISBN 978-93-5206-830-2

Dedication

*This Infinite ocean of Light, **Para Brahma**, the Supreme God.*

I'd like to thank my parents for allowing me to follow my ambitions throughout my career.

My thanks and love go to my wife Shreelata and my children Kartik and Pranab, who forgave me for stealing so much time from them to write this book. I hope that one day they can read this book and understand why I spent so much time being social, helping people and reading books.

My sincere thanks to Christopher Burchett's for his initial editing of my book. His editorial suggestions after reading the first draft of this book were most valuable.

My heartfelt thanks go to Mamta Agrawal, the main editor of my book for her expertise and devotion while editing and also my sincere gratitude to J.S. Ishwarya for helping in the process editing.

My deep appreciation goes to all of the others, here and there, who have made this book possible.

Contents

About Jagadeesh Pillai

Jagadeesh Pillai a voracious reader, writer and a true research scholar was born in Varanasi, the abode of Lord Shiva. He is a multi faceted polymath with innate qualities, creative ideas and many remarkable achievements. Although his roots extend back to "Gods own Country" (Kerala), the residents of Varanasi feel proud about him and adore him as a child of Varanasi who caters to every individual in need without any expectations. A deep study into his profile reflects that he has added so many feathers to his cap which make him quite unique. He is a Guinness Book of World Record Holder for "Script to Screen" which he achieved by producing and directing a state of art animation film within the shortest time possible by breaking the earlier set record by a Canadian. There are many National and International Awards and recognitions to his credit.

It is hard to believe that he has produced and directed more than 100 Documentaries on a particular city (Varanasi), all executed single-handedly.

A multifaceted person who can apply the best of his calibre and acumen using his inborn talents which have been showered upon every human being granting them an immense capacity to learn, experience and experiment many things and do wonders in this world of discrimination and disparities.

He is a teacher and a student at the same time who always learns and teaches every day. As a master, his weakness is that he never sticks to a particular subject. Perhaps this weakness gives him the strength to master any area which he comes across.

Each of his day is dawned with learning a new topic and he spends most of his time experimenting and researching with it.

He is a selfless social activist and a motivational speaker too.

He also has a life full of struggle, ups and downs and failures like any other human being in this modern age. But he never gave up and faced all his trials and tribulations with extreme confidence, which made him a man of letters, confidence with a rich practical knowledge and experience.

Foreword

In The Moments when I met God, Dr. Jagadeesh Pillai explains how the hidden power of helping others can empower you to grow rich in every sense of the word, in love, in wealth, in happiness, in health, and yes, in your own communication and relationship with God. He gives examples which suggest that we need not be deterred by everyday problems of life. If we are internally strong and have faith in God, external setbacks and forces cannot keep us down for long. The examples and stories cited in the book are real life experiences of the writer.

This book will help ignite love for helping others which, in turn, will help uncover our special talents and then utilize those talents to become all we can be. If we follow the right track in our lives, the opportunity comes our way sooner or later; our plans are intuitionally conveyed to God, who sends appropriate help to us. All we need is to recognize the openings and move accordingly. This book bridges action and vision, helps us leverage our time, talent and personal excellence, deepen our faith in God and thus change our vision into reality.

Dr. Karan Singh

New Delhi – 110 021

Tuesday 17 November 2015

Note: *His highness Dr. Karan Singh is a Padma Vibhushan Awardee by Government of India, Member of Parliament, Chancellor of Banaras Hindu University and author of many books.*

Preface

"The Moments When I met God"

God is probably the most used word in the world.

There are many myths, religions and beliefs prevalent in our society related to God. Based on them, there are temples, churches, mosques and many such places where one can feel the divinity of God. Still knowing and understanding God is a mystery.

Believers and non-believers all have a question about its existence, shape, form etc. and even if there exists a form how can one perceive it.

Different religions name God in different manner and therefore all religions have assigned different nomenclatures to God and many different stories have been created related to Him.

No one has seen nor understands his real form. But the faith in God is blind. The reason is that everyone believes there is an omnipotent and omnipresent power that is ruling the world.

People have different concepts of God and according to me where all those concepts of God meet, the real God manifests.

Whenever I need motivation, a helping hand and to take wise decisions, I take recourse to God and my concept of God has manifested in various occasion/situations in my life. These manifestations have helped me in my life to become successful and have changed me from a common man to an uncommon with multiple talents, knowledge, experience, name, fame, health, wealth & prosperity, all that I longed for in my life.

In this book, I wish to share my experience and my realization of those manifestations. The concept of God, the realization of God and the manifestations of Him in different forms may differ/vary from person to person.

Jagadeesh Pillai

Chapter 1

Understanding God

I have started writing this book with the headline "Understanding God" because there are millions of people who have deep faith on God. They are sincerely devoted and have no problem in donating any amount every day in the name of God. But the problem is lack of knowledge or understanding what and who God is. They simply follow myths as per the tenets of their religion with its symbolic representation of God. Everybody believes that God has immense power or one can say, He is omnipotent and can change anything within a fraction of a second. We see many people around us who are sincere in their life as well as devoted to God. They regularly pray with full devotion but still no miracle actually happens in their lives.

Suppose there is an employee devoted to God and he prays every day. Still throughout his life he has never seen a significant raise in his life or a big positive change in his career, rather he has had to face ups and downs as usual like everybody. Whatever happens, good or bad, the faith in God never diminishes. If one of our dearest and nearest does not accept our request or rejects anything, we immediately feel bad about them or sometime we even discontinue our relation with them. But in the case of God, this rarely happens and we continue to believe in Him with even deepest faith. Is this because we love God or we fear Him?

You can even imagine many people in your surroundings; you can say they are good people because of their attitude and devotion towards God. But life moves on a fixed time table much like a movie continues as scripted and directed by the director. The actors imagine and perform so many actions while shooting the movie, but the final movie is completed as per the decisions of the director.

The situation is not always the same with everyone. We, the actors, can change the script, and also the role we play in the movie, if we have a close relation and understanding with the Director. The similar thing happens with God also. If you understand God and if you know the proper communication method with God, you too can rise from any level to higher levels or I mean, God can do miracles for you.

It is not wrong to believe that there is somebody who has created the universe, earth, humans, animals and so many other living and non-living beings. We can call Him the "Creator." People from different religions have given different name to that "Creator." For the spiritual people, this existence of a creator is a fact. Though known by different names in different religions and in different languages, ultimately the vibration of the word goes to that one Creator. For example, let's take the word "Water." The Hindi speaking people will say "Jal," Malayalam speaking people will say "Vellam," Tamil speaking people will say "Tanni" and in Sanskrit is "Jalam," Ab is Arabic. There are hundreds of words in different languages for "Water." Just see the difference. The word is different, spelling is different, pronunciation is different but ultimately they all refer to one element "water." People when hear the word for water in their language, their imagination will go to that particular element only. It is the same with God too.

Each and everybody, whether an atheist or a theist, has faith in God. An atheist will also become in devoted to God while undergoing an extreme miserable period of life of in his life. When he meets a strange situation in life that is beyond his control, he will definitely remember the Supreme Spirit, may be for a second.

If we refer somebody or some object and tell that this is God, no one would ever believe in it. Even if he believes, he will carry certain doubts in his mind.

Let's take a look at an example.

If there is an announcement that next Sunday in the city stadium some particular God would appear in the sky for a few minutes to see and bless everybody. What will happen? Will everybody in the city believe this? Should we expect all the people to go to the stadium to see the God? No? Elder brother of a family will tell his younger brother to look after the shop so that he can go and check what's happening. Not in the extreme belief that he will definitely see the real God.

And the day comes. We expect 50% of the people of the city will flock to the stadium to see God. Suddenly some lightening flashes in the sky and a God form appears, like we see in films or dramas. He blesses everybody and sprinkles some holy water drops on all the persons and disappears. What would be the situation after that? Will all the 50% of the crowd would believe it? People will start discussing so many myths and stories. Even if some people have strong belief in Him, others may confused them. Somebody will say that it is the magic of some magician and not God.

I mean, even if the God in photos appears in real life, we are not going to believe it. But still the faith in Him continues.

It might be the real God. But, how shall we confirm it? That's why I have started with this chapter "Understanding God.' If you don't understand the form of God, you won't be able to identifying him, when he is in front of you. My aim is to make you understand various form in which God appears. We have to only understand and recognize Him.

We must have a clear picture about God because we have blind faith in Him. So, forget about visualizing God, let's understand God.

Chapter 2

Concept of God

How the concept of God has developed over the years has always been an intriguing question for most of us. Whatever concept or idea that we bear in our mind regarding God is just hypothetical as the range of belief is differ from individual to individual, religion to religion and tradition to tradition.

Hence we follow what we have been taught; we have seen and learnt since our childhood. As I have mentioned all of us belong to a particular religion and follow that with the character from of God as perceived in that religion.

For hundreds and thousands of years, people have been debating whether God really exists or not and it is concluded that the answer to this unanswerable query lies in the abstract philosophy. The innumerable religions in the world have tried to concretise the form of God through various objects like wood, stone and other available materials, but there is no authentic evidence available till date that affirms his shape and form.

But what is the most common concept of God that we bear in our mind?

1. God loves everybody on the earth.
2. God watches us every time and takes care of us.
3. God blesses us, if we are positive and punishes us if we are negative in our karma.

4. The Universe is a creation of God.
5. Each and every thing that occurs in our life is according to His wish.
6. When there is no near and dear one to help, God helps.
7. God gives wealth and prosperity.
8. God assists us in difficult times.
9. God is with us every time and everywhere.

And the list of different concept continues like this....

Let us take a look at the life style of some people in our society.

A man gets up early in the morning, makes proper prayers and goes to his office on time and does his work sincerely. As per his concept, God is ruling us and if he does positive work he will always get positive results in his life and whatever good things are there in his life are the blessings from God.

A second person, probably a Government Employee, who too makes his prayers probably much more than the above person but he accepts bribes from the clients who visit his office for a purpose. But according to his concept, he believes, if he spends more time on prayers, God will clear him of his sins of taking bribes.

There is a third person who has built a grand temple in the garden of his own house itself and every day in the morning before going to his textile shop; he makes prayers and rituals in a very expensive way. And when he is in the shop, his eyes are on the crowd pushing along the roads and he always hints his staff to attract the clients and bring them inside his shop. He opens his money locker many times in a day and counts the money. Now it has become his habit to count the money collected and he feels satisfied. But still he is eager to increase the collection through new clients visiting his shop.

Business and making money are an essential part of life but some people are addicted to it. He does not pay much to his staff or even pay to his beggars, but he spends money on God in his own temple built at home. It's his concept of God.

Once, I asked my four year old son, whether he knows about God or not? He immediately pointed to a calendar and showed me a picture and said, yes that is God. Then again I asked, how you can say it's God, he is a man like us wearing some makeup. He said, no I am confident that this is a picture God with more powers than human being because when he is afraid he calls God and he becomes fearless. It's the concept or thought form he has created or built up in his mind in 4 years. Obviously, he has understood and follows what he has learned from us.

So the concept of God is different for different people or people create the concept of God as per their necessities or priorities in their life.

Whatever it is, one thing is sure that where all these concepts meet, God is manifested.

Just imagine, did you ever have a meeting with God whenever your concept of God was manifested?

Yes, you have met God in reality. But you ignored it because your understanding about God was not clear.

Let's clear the confusion and let's experience the real form of God.

Chapter 3

Visualising God

This is a very important chapter of this book, because here I will attempt to help one visualize God through the eyes of a common man.

We have to consider that just one world, one kind of human being and one God is there. Let others give different names and make divisions. But we should only concentrate and understand the Super-Natural Power of God. Nowhere the name works, but what works is power.

One cannot disagree about the Super-Natural Power of God because in this world and also in this life there are so many natural phenomena that occur for example: Breathing, internal functions of body, the rising and setting of the sun, rain, birth, death, the list goes on. No human being can manage these things. So if things happen without our knowledge or without any involvement of man, certainly, there is some supreme power who manages all these phenomenon and controlling them.

Here I reckon and incident that I would like to cite. I had an Italian friend, Fabio who very often visited India and whenever I met him, he was dressed in white from top to bottom. He came to India with a group of people from Italy and his intention was to visit an Ashram in India. Before I met him, he had already visited one or two ashrams. He did not intend to join any ashram but his intention was to find answers to a few questions. He thought somebody from an

Indian Ashram could satiate his thirst for knowledge. But he was wrong.

I was introduced to him through one of my musician friends at a musical concert by virtue of my association with some spiritual organization, social service and charity programmes.

But what astonished me were his questions. His question was about God. Whether God exists or not & if He exists where is God, Where can we see God? were some of his queries. I was quite confused. How could I help him because he needed full proof answers from such a person whom he could blindly believe and be satisfied with the answers.

He never asked me to search for a scholar and anybody for his help, because he himself was searching for such a person.

The next day, according to his request, I accompanied him to visit the city, streets and the bank of the Ganges etc. During this journey, he found a person who could answer his questions. It was a teacher who was returning from the Ganges after a holy bath. He excitedly said, I have found the person, he can answer me. I was so confused because I had already referred him to many such persons and scholars during the previous days looking much better than this guy and he has already rejected all of them. After a long thought, my sixth sense could not even find out why he had chosen that particular guy or why was he inclined towards that particular person.

We followed that guy to find out where he lived. His place was just a few minutes away from the Ganges. He sought my help to meet that person to ask his questions.

But my astonished mind was still searching for the answer as to why he had chosen this person. Finally I asked him.

His answer was really interesting. He said, "Yesterday in front of a church, I found him praying to the Lord. While strolling on the streets the another day, I found him praying in front of a mosque and today in the morning, I saw him praying in front of a temple."

According to Fabio, those who believe in one God and respect all religions will be the right person to ask his questions about God.

Finally, I decided to meet that person and we arrived there. He was about to give some spiritual teaching to the students present there. I introduced Fabio to him and also told him the reason for our interest in meeting him. The scholar welcomed us with a smile and we sat on the mat placed there.

After making his preparation, the scholar came and sat near us. Looking at Fabio he asked, "So you have some questions and you are expecting answers from me right?"

"Yes.... Guruji"...Fabio used this word "Guruji" to address him.

The scholar continued "Then before you start asking questions, I have one question."

"Sure Guruji..... What is it?" asked Fabio surprisingly.

Guruji: "Don't you really know the answer to your questions?"

Fabio: "No Guruji...that is why..?" Before continuing, Guruji said "Yes..that's why you have come to me."

Fabio: "Ya."

Guruji: "But if you believe that I can answer your questions, then you too know the answers."

Fabio: "I didn't get you, Guruji."

Guruji: "I will make you understand. But I too will ask some questions after answering your questions and you have to answer me sincerely"

Fabio: "Sure..Guruji.... I will try my best."

Guruji: "Ok then.. what is your first question?"

Fabio: "My first question is, whether God really exists or did he exist?"

Guruji: "Good Question. Which country do you belong to?"

Fabio: "Italy."

Guruji: "Whom do you or your country people worship the most there?"

Fabio: "Obviously, we worship Lord Jesus."

Guruji: "So, probably the people there go to Church, right?"

Fabio: "Yes"

Guruji: "You too.."

Fabio: "Yes..of course, me too"

Guruji: "Why?"

Fabio (confused): "Oh God....difficult question"

Guruji: "You have to say what forced your mind to go to the church, why don't you prefer to go to watch a movie that time instead of going to the church. Of course, movie will entertain you a lot. But if you have chosen to spend time in the church, something must have forced you."

Fabio was unable to answer.

Guruji: "So.... In my question, you are the guy who visited the church by some force, and therefore only you can answer me why did you go there and what forced you to go there?"

Fabio: "Guruji..it's really hard to say, but what I can say is that I felt some spiritual meditation, relaxed mind or I was at peace when I was there."

Guruji: "Let me also add that your were calm, less angry, less envious but filled with joy and peace."

Fabio: "Yes Guruji."

Guruji: "In short at least during that time you felt divine, spiritual, secure and you were filled with positive energy..... Am I right?"

"Yes Guruji".... Fabio affirmed what Guruji said but was still in a confused state that was reflected on his face.

Guruji: "If there is no church or a place like a church in the world, what will happen? Will you feel relaxed? Will you be able to meditate and will you feel spiritual, divine or peaceful?"

Fabio: "No Guruji."

Guruji: "So if there is something like a church, where you can open your heart, confess, get relaxation, feel positive energy...then surely there is something beyond our imagination and control that is ruling us, is it true or not?

Fabio (innocently): "True."

Guruji: "Then what is the truth? Does God exist or doesn't he ?"

Fabio: "It's still not clear but I agree some power is there that holds the reigns of this world and our life."

Guruji: "Can you name that power?"

Fabio said: "No…"

Guruji: "If your answer is NO, don't you think we should give a name to that something, because in the universe there is a name for everything, even for you too?"

Fabio: "Yes, of course."

Guruji: "So what name will suit that 'divine' something"?

Fabio (with confidence): "God."

Guruji: "Are you sure?"

Fabio: "Yes…Guruji."

Guruji: "So tell me now, who has given the answer to your question, me or you?

Fabio: "Me…, but of course, through you."

Guruji: "What is your next question?"

Fabio: "Who is a 'Guru' ?"

Guruji (with a smile): "Why you are calling me "Guruji" if you don't know the meaning of Guru?"

Fabio: "Yes…because in India, everybody addresses in the similar way a scholar like you, as Guruji, so I am also addressing you."

Guruji: "Ok…then let it be like that" then he continued, "you had a question about God's existence and for the answer, you came here all the way from Italy in search of a person and finally you have chosen me. But in fact you knew the answer of your question. I have just felt your thoughts and feelings and tried to change the way you think. So tell me why you could find answer to your questions in my presence rather what extra ordinary do you see in me?"

Fabio (replied after a little thought): "Your way of thinking, your way of making me understand and of course your spiritual knowledge."

Guruji: "No need to go such a big explanation, just say that he who helped you to understand you and your thoughts in a better manner is a Guru."

Guruji: "Everybody has some questions and of course they know the answers too. But still they are unknown to it and when they meet a Guru they get a chance to exercise their thoughts and they start understanding themselves better."

"Can you predict your tomorrow, what will happen exactly? No…we are nobody to make our tomorrow's time table. There is someone or something who controls us. So, as you said if we have to give a name to that something, it is God."

This discussion between Fabio and Guruji continued for a few hours with different questions. If necessary, I will continue the same in the forthcoming chapters.

So it was really an interesting experience with Fabio and Guruji.

Now I will cite another story. This story is about a king who was successfully ruling his kingdom. He was always doing good things for the betterment of the people of his kingdom.

Once he set out on a tour to the streets and villages of his kingdom to meet people, to know their needs and to see their living style. During his tour, he noticed that there were many temples on every street. People were worshipping God and were performing some rites and rituals. Out of inquisitiveness, the king asked his people whom they were worshipping. All the people were happy thinking that the king was concerned about them. They replied by referring God with different names and praised Him enthusiastically. The king was so confused and irritated that he stopped his tour and immediately returned to his palace.

He immediately called a meeting of all the scholars of his kingdom for a discussion on this issue. Everybody reached within few hours. The King posed a strange question in front of the mand the question was

"I am the King of this Kingdom. I feed people, I rule over the people, I educate the people, I punish the people for their wrong doings, I provide everything, but why do people worship somebody else as God and why not me? I want to see God and I want to know what is so special about God?"

In rage, he ordered the scholars present there to make arrangements for him to meet GOD within two days. This order created an anxiety among the scholars and frightened them too.

They looked at each other with questions as to what had happened to the King, what non sense he was talking, how can one show him the real God. If the scholars failed to show him God, they would be punished severely. They thought about it day and night. They lost their sleep, thirst and hunger and it took a toll on their health.

After two days, the time came when all the scholars had to assemble at the same place in front of the king. The king could guess from their facial expression that they were all afraid of the consequences as they could not find God in concrete form and shape to bring along with them to the palace. Hence, the image or visualization of God still remained an abstract concept for king. As expected, the king seethed with rage and as he was about to announce the punishment to the scholars, a scholar stood up and said that he would show him the concrete form of God. All other scholars were taken aback to see the guts of this scholar. Some thought it was his nonsense that he was trying to show God to the king. Some of them felt relaxed thinking that if he succeeds in showing God to the king, they will also get the chance to see God. Apart from that, they will be saved from the punishment too.

The scholar requested the king to come into the open garden at 12 noon so that he could see God. The king readily agreed and was happy.

As decided, at 12 noon, the King came in the open garden along with the scholar who promised to show him God. All other scholars also came there. But it was too hot because it was noon and the sun was at its zenith. The scholar requested the king to come in the centre of the garden and focus his sight on the sun for a few seconds. It was only after that he can see God in concrete form.

The king was happy to hear that. Immediately, he came in the centre of the garden and tried his best to focus on the centre of the sun. But within in a second, the King changed his sight from the sun and started looking down to earth. He told the scholar that he could not focus on the sun even for a second, because of its powerful rays and bright light.

The scholar smiled and told the king, "This powerful, bright and burning sun is a very little part or a particle of that God whom you wish to see. If you fail to comprehend this fact, how do you intend to see the complete form of God? Hence, at first you have to understand and see God as He is present in all his natural creations." The king realized the hidden truth and the scholar explained him more about God and the universe.

The scholar also reminded him of his own confession which he made two days ago after visiting the streets that he was fed up the people of his Kingdom. The Scholar corrected the King and told him that he did not provide the air we breathe, the carbon-dioxide the plants breathe, the sun light, and the water etc. Many kingdoms, many universe, many sun, unlimited stars are there and all these are not in our control. We are also a part of this Universe like plants, animals and millions of living and non-living beings on the earth.

✦ ✦ ✦

As my intention is to help every common man to visualize God, the citations of above stories are necessary.

Now I would like to start with the most important part of this book and therefore, I would cite a real incident where I have not just felt God but I realized God. Probably, this is the only way to see and understand God. Let me share my experience in this regard. I am sure that after reading this experience most of the people will understand God in real sense. They will be able to recall moments when they have manifested God and they will immediately understand when God comes in front of them in the future.

My sales tax advocate, Mr. Mahesh Gupta (Maheshji we called him), a very deep and faith in God. He got up early in the morning and performed pooja (worshipping God) for hours at his home every day. Then he visited nearby temples before he got ready for his office. His chamber was approximately 10 kilometer away from his house. On his way from his home to office, whenever he saw a temple, he would get down from his scooter and would go to the temple. On any happening, he would not miss letting out his expletive "sab maya ka ichaa hai" which means "everything happens in illusion" or we can say "it's the wish of some divine magical power." Why did he use this phrase without any relevance, I didn't know and I kept wondering. But I think he used that phrase more than 100 times in a day. After few years, I could imagine why he used that phrase while talking. What I could understand was his blind faith in God and his profession. As I have mentioned earlier, he is an advocate by profession and at the same time he is a sincere devotee of God. He often faces professional problems. He has to charge excess from his clients for his services being an advocate. Actually it is a part and parcel of his profession. But being a sincere devotee of God, he is afraid of God for charging that extra money from the clients. To satisfy himself or for his mental balance, he blames God saying that the world and he himself are Maya (illusion) and this is happening according to God's wish. He feels that he is doing crime charging extra from his clients. But he has no other option, he is an advocate and it's a part of his profession.

We stop with the story of Mr. Gupta and will continue with it later.

✦ ✦ ✦

Now I will cite another incident of the same period.

My wife received an invitation to attend a spiritual function from her colleagues on a Sunday. But we were unaware of the purpose of that function. Even, on Sundays my wife has to go for her duty. Therefore she requested me to attend that function on her behalf. Frankly speaking, I was not in a mood to attend but for the sake of formality, I planned to go and decided to spend a few minutes there and then come back.

When I reached there, I became late by an hour and the function was about to be finish. It was a kind of group that served the society under a spiritual leader and organized sat sangs (meeting of a group of spiritual people for praising God and their Guru). People chanted hymns and spiritual songs in praise of God and Guru. I was really impressed to see this activity and the atmosphere there and I cursed myself for being late.

At the same place I was with one of my friends, Uday. I inquired about his intention behind attending such a spiritual gathering. He told me that this group organized such gatherings every week and following it they serve poor, needy and under privileged people etc.

The turning point came, when he told me about his visit to nearby Mother Teresa Mission few weeks ago with his mother. Mother Teresa Mission is like a hospital with 100 bed capacity near the Ganges. The followers of Mother Teresa and nuns of this mission bring unwanted people who are ill and are abandoned by family or those who have nobody to look after them and are left suffering on the streets in pain to the mission. The mission takes care of their basic needs like food, shelter and clothes and also takes care of their treatment which is provided free of cost.

Then I asked him, why he visited that place.

He said that he took some fruits and vegetables to the mission as a sort of small contribution from his side.

Though, his action was admirable, I was unhappy because he was also one of the members of the group who actually organized that spiritual function whose main motto was service. He should mention the group about the necessities of Mother Teresa Mission and as a group they would do lot together.

After hearing that, I was very eager to visit the mission and requested him to take me there the next Sunday.

As planned, next Sunday around 9 O'clock we arrived there. The gate man asked us our names and purpose of visit and mentioned it in the register. We went inside to seek permission from the in charge for going inside. We got permission. As I entered into the first floor on the left side I saw many very sick men in different beds. The gate man was watching my expression and told me in a sad and feeble voice that they are counting their last breath of life. There were TB patients, leprosy patients, AIDS patients, etc.

We, then, directly went to the guest room to meet the duty sister and sought her permission because only after getting a green signal from her, we could enter the rooms or anywhere inside to meet the patients. In a few minutes, the duty sister came and she took us to each and every room. There were many sections - ladies ward, gents ward, children's ward and a separate ward for patients who were in critical condition. But none of the patients had arrived there **on their own**. All had been brought from the streets in the mission's vehicle. All these patients had no kith & kin of their own to look after them. They all followed different religions and all of them were equal there and were treated on equal terms. Hence no one could make out the religion to which they belonged to.

A miracle happened to me there. I entered each and every room without any hesitation. My habit till that day had been to stay away from such places even from hospitals. I rejected these types of places. It was a very unpleasant thing for me staying at these places even for a couple of minutes because the sight of unhappy and painful faces, helplessness of people, the hidden agony, foul smell, medicines etc. made me displeased.

That day, I happily entered the rooms. I even touched many patients who had wounds on their hands or legs, very affectionately. The duty sister prohibited me from entering certain sections where there were people in a critical condition with contagious diseases. For me it was really like a miracle. My mind had totally changed, I didn't notice any bad odours there. The patients were looking at me with tear dried eyes and with a sad face. They might be thinking that somebody has come to their rescue.

After visiting all the wards, we came back to the sister's room to discuss certain issues there.

She explained everything to me. She also told us that the mission used to get a lot of charity from different places in the form of money, food, clothes, etc. and most of the helping hands were foreign tourists. But after the World Trade Center attack in US that time, only a few tourists were there to help them and because of shortage of medicines available to them.

Then I asked sister what was the most necessary item there which you get less as charity. She said medicines. I requested her to give me a list of medicines she wanted. She provided me the same and I promised her that I will try to collect the maximum medicines from the list and would meet her again very soon.

I tried to procure medicines through different sources. My sister in law helped me with a bundle of medicines in one month. One of my other friends, Jamal Bhai who was working with me suggested to share this information amongst all of our friends and to collect unused, unexpired medicines available at their houses.

Through many such campaigns, I was able to collect a lot of medicines than I had ever expected. Frankly speaking, not a single medicine was there as contribution from my end or my wife. I had not spent even a single penny for that. But, I had a big bundle of medicines to donate to Mother Teresa Mission. The biggest contributor of medicines for the Mission was my sister-in-law, Shrilekha."

The next Sunday, I went there to handover all the medicines to the sister in the Mission.

✦ ✦ ✦

I will continue with the story of Mr. Mahesh Gupta (advocate), the blind believer in God and who was also afraid of God.

The next morning I called Mahesh Gupta and asked some strange questions. It was like I was joking him in the morning over the phone, but I was a bit serious in my talk.

I asked Mr. Gupta, "You are a blind believer of God and you sincerely worship God every day for many hours than many of us. Have you ever seen the real GOD?"

First he laughed and asked me the most expected question "Why are you joking in the morning?."

I told him that I was very serious and had no intention of cracking jokes.

With a lack of interest in my question, he just answered that he can see God in pictures hung there and in temples.

I said, "They are somebody else's imagination, portrait and sculptures. Will they speak to you? Will they come in front of you?"

Mr. Gupta was unsure and said, "No."

I could not stop myself and asked him why he was confident about the existence and real form of God.

Sensing his nonplussed state, I offered to show him the real God.

Again he questioned me, "Why are you joking in the morning?"

I reaffirmed myself and said, "I can show you the real God."

In a serious tone, he asked "how can you do that?" His attitude was changed by this time, and felt that I was not joking. He was aware that I was also engaged in God worshipping and spiritual activities. I was not an atheist. So something is there that he could smell.

Then he asked me to show him the real God.

I told him that on the following Sunday around 10 O'clock, I would take him to a place which would change his perception.

As it was a matter related to God, he agreed to spare a few hours with me, though half heartedly.

It was Sunday and in the morning, on that day, I once again invited Mr. Gupta to come to my home.

Mr. Gupta came to my house on time. I also took the bundle of medicines that I collected for Mother Teresa Mission and we started our journey in my car, on the way, we picked up Uday also. He had already informed Mother Teresa Mission over the phone about our arrival with medicines.

In half an hour, we reached at the Mission. They were about to finish their morning prayer as we entered. In that big hall, most of the patients were standing there and their eyes were watching at us, the visitors.

Mr. Gupta was totally confused and asked me why we had come to this place as he visited that place for the first time. I think he felt bad. But I signaled him to wait for a few more minutes.

After the prayer was over, the sister came to us and she introduced us to all the patients gathered there. They all gave us a warm welcome by folding their hands. Their faces were filled with sorrow, but at the same time they were expressing their gratitude to us because they were aware that visitors like us might have brought something for their welfare.

Now it was time to explain everything to Mr. Gupta and to show him the final picture. I promised to the sister to bring the medicines for the patients and also had promised Mr. Gupta to show him GOD.

I explained all this to Mr. Gupta.

I told him that we were at the Mother Teresa Mission; the world recognized MOTHER who had won the Noble Prize for peace. We are witnessing here a small part of her vide charity service activities she started and spread all over the world.

I told Mr. Gupta that the sisters here are followers of Mother Teresa who have dedicated their lives in the service of mankind. These patients are from different parts of the country, follow different religions and have different temperament. Here at the mission, no one is discriminated on basis of the religion that he/she follows. Everyone is treated equally and is given due respect and love. The sisters and her colleagues move out in search on the streets and bring those people who are abandoned by society, left at the mercy of fate, thrown away by someone and are very badly suffering from some disease or living a miserable life. They might had belonged a good family in the past.

The sister and her team who follow Mother Teresa's path never asked the name or religion while lending a helping hand to the patients who are admitted in the mission. They happily adopt them and bring them to the Mission to provide the basic amenities.

The experience of visualizing the real God starts from here...

Showing the group of patients who were standing in front of us, I asked Mr. Gupta to identify their religion. It was an extraordinary difficult task for him as there is only one religion, only one caste that is "HUMANITY."

Giving due respect to Mr. Gupta, as he was older than my friend Uday and me, I handed over the bundle of medicine to Mr. Gupta. Further, I requested him to hand it over to the sister who stood in front but in the presence of all those patients. Mr. Gupta was left speechless. As requested by us, he stepped ahead and handed over the bundle to the sister. All the patients there were looking at Mr. Gupta with extreme gratitude. Their eyes were filled with tears and with their joined hands, they thanked Mr. Gupta for his kindness and help. Uday and I were standing behind him.

Slowly I stepped ahead and moved towards Mr. Gupta. He was standing with a pale face and in a totally confused state of mind, a situation he could never have imagined.

I whispered in his ear. "Mr. Gupta, did you see something?." He looked at me and was unable to say anything. I felt that he was not in a position to say anything.

I said, "Mr. Gupta I brought you here to show you God. As I promised you and I kept my promise. The God is present here. He slowly moved his face here and there in search of God.

I said, "Mr. Gupta, go and look deep into the tear-filled eyes of these patients. You will see the multiple reflections of God in their eyes and the form of God in their heart. Those patients see God in their eyes and if you look into their eyes closely you can also see the God whom they are watching.

They are seeing their God in front of them with a bundle of medicines to cure them. In brief, what they are seeing in their eyes, what they are feeling in their heart, is the real GOD, Mr. Gupta, you are God now."

"People like you, people like Mother Teresa, people like these sisters and other staff of this Mission who have devoted their life to the service of these helpless people and mankind are real God."

I saw his eyes welled with tears.

One needs extreme physical, mental and spiritual strength in his trying times especially when a person is alone and there is no one to lend a helping hand. Facing misfortunes which often come in battalions take a heavy toll on him and the most popular belief of the present day that gives him some solace is - God is good all the time and He loves everybody. Others console him by saying that God takes care of those who have nobody to fall back on. In the deepest core of our heart, even we feel, this is a passing phase of our life and God is never wrong. He is doing the right thing.

This is the reason why I mentioned in the first chapter of the book that we need knowledge to understand God.

Often we get help from our friends and relatives which goes un-noticed and we take it in our stride. We fail to conceive or accept that the permanence of love attained through mutuality is a beautiful idea. We fail to understand the difference between life of love and life without love.

Chapter 4

The Form of God

In the previous chapters we have experienced the ways to visualize and understand God. Still there lingers is a question about the form of God. In what form does God come to us? God is omnipresent and omnipotent. But we are unable to perceive His form because of our ignorance or illusion.

I will try to explain in my own way with the help of the following story.

While strolling along the road in the evening, I saw a man who looked like a beggar lying on the road side. His face was almost covered with beard and he gave a cruel, threatening and bad look. There were sores on his body. His facial expression revealed that he was experiencing severe pain because of his untreated sores, hunger and thirst. The pain had made him immobile too. With tear filled eyes, he was begging help from the passers-by, but not a single person payed heed to him which made him even more dejected.

Owing to his weird and threatening expression, and strange looks people felt that he was a cruel man or a criminal. He might be a thief; he might be a pickpocket or he might have indulged into wrong deeds in his life. But this is just a wild guess that we are making.

If we look at him closely, we can understand that he was really in need of some help and at least needed a glass of water. But nobody sympathized with him.

Joining his hands together, he begged people on the road and sometimes he looked at the sky as if he was praying to God for help in his hour of need.

Thinking of the beggar as a person of ill-doings, some reject him or do not even look at him. One tends to think why will God help such a bad person?

And yes, you are right in thinking so.

At this moment you see, he is in a very sorry state, in a very miserable condition. Perhaps, this situation is the repercussion of his sins done in the past. But at this time his prayer to God is sincere. He may not be requesting God to save him and help him so that he can continue his life as he wrongly lived in the past. Rather he may be confessing to God for whatever wrong he might have done in the past. And now when he is in extreme pain, his prayer is sincere and his mind is innocent.

We often come across so many people in society with muscle power and money power. They always try to cheat others and collect money and properties by virtue of their power. When they have the power of money, they have body guards and they roam like kings thinking that all others are under their feet. I have also seen such a person in my life and his painful death too.

A couple of years back, I purchased a piece of land in a colony. When I planned to begin the construction, I came to know that the brother of the colonizer was the supplier of bricks, soil, cement etc., and it was compulsory to procure these raw materials from him at the rate which he quoted. To my utter surprise, the rates quoted by the brother of the colonizer were higher than the market. They also had a condition that If anybody purchases the material from outside to build his house, he would punish him very badly. So I decided to drop the plan of building my house there and quietly sold the land.

A few years later, I came to know that the brother of colonizer was seriously injured and admitted to the medical college hospital because he had met with an accident. He was in the ICU for many weeks and expired later, after suffering a lot. While he was in the hospital he looked like a child, neither his muscle power nor money power proved to be of any help to him in such a critical situation.

Now, let us revert to the incident of road side beggar who was suffering from pain and was praying sincerely for help. There were many shops near him. He requested each of the shopkeeper for help but nobody really believed him that he was indeed. His prayer continued.

After some time, a shopkeeper took pity on his miserable condition and decided to help him. He got some water and biscuits from his shop and gave it to the beggar. The beggar was delighted and his eyes gleamed with joy. He quickly took the water and started drinking. Then he opened the packet of biscuit and started eating as if he had seen it for the first time in his life. While drinking water and eating biscuits, tears welled up in his eyes. He felt satiated and relaxed. With folded hands and tear filled eyes, he thanked the shop keeper profusely.

The shopkeeper feeling blessed and went back to his shop.

The aim of citing this story of a painful roadside beggar and the shop keeper was to show the form of God.

Here I am reminded of a quote from Bhagavad Gita. "The power of God is with you at all times through the activities of mind, senses, breathing and emotions and He is constantly doing all the work using "you" as a mere instrument."

We usually say "God is Love?." Exactly, the form of God that worked here was LOVE. Not only here, every where God appears in the form of Love.

There were so many people walking on the same street and there were so many shop keepers also. The beggar had been suffering his pain for many hours. But it is surprising that only one shopkeeper came there to help. In his heart, some kind of love, affection or mercy had been generated. It was actually not the person as a shopkeeper who worked there, but the kindness originated in his heart towards that beggar forced him to go and help. In another words we can say God appeared in the form of Love in the heart of the shopkeeper and that Love towards the beggar ultimately forced that shopkeeper to go to the road side beggar and help him.

Suppose, instead of Love, had anger or hatred dominated in the heart of the shop keeper like many other people on the road, the beggar could not have got help. This is symbolic of "Love is God."

We are all aware of Mother Teresa, who was saintly figure for underprivileged people.

It was the Love form of God in the heart of Mother Teresa that forced her to help the poor and the ignored people, who lived on the streets.

It was the "Love as God" that forced us to support the mission with medicines.

It was the "Love as God" that forced Uday to go there and provide food and fruits to the needy.

It was the "Love as God" in the sisters and other staff of Mother Teresa Mission that forced them to serve mankind.

It means when love flows from our heart towards others, we can say that God is there in our heart too.

I hope the form of God is clear. But it is my way of visualizing and thinking as a common man.

Remember, love, kindness, compassion, empathy will never be wasted. These virtues always hold importance in our life and make a difference which no one can even imagine. And yes, they bless the receiver as well as the giver.

Chapter 5

Prayer to God

You are already blessed, that is why you are here as a Human.

Most of the people pray to God for their well being, or for the betterment of their family and children and for many other reasons. I also had a habit of praying with a big list in the past. "Oh God, I need this, I need that" After a few years I have changed way of praying to God. I had learned many thing from Nature (universe) that forced me to change my style of praying to God.

Let me cite an instance:

Suppose, there are two people sitting in the same prayer hall Mr. A and Mr. B, and there is one more person Mr. C, who is not in the prayer hall.

Mr. A is silently praying to God.

"My God, please take care of my wife, my children; please help my business prosper. Give excellent grades to my children. God help me grow more than my competitors or my neighbors. Help me progress by leaps and bounds."

Mr. B is also silently praying to God

"My God, you are great. Please give good health, wealth and peace to Mr. C. He is a great man. Because of his mercy, my family and I are enjoying a good life. He is a good boss. He also helped my son to get admission in a good school. He takes good care of us and all other employees. Please let him prosper day by day and let us live under his protective shadow."

You might be wondering whose prayer God might have accepted. My intuition says of Mr. B. His prayer was sincere and transparent. He asked nothing for himself. He prayed for the well being of Mr. C, who is probably the boss of the company where he works.

But Mr. A prayed for himself and his family only. He also prayed to let him grow more than others. His mind was selfish while praying and selfishness is a negative quality and I don't think, this a proper way of to pray.

So, I think it is better to do something to create more people like Mr. B who pray differently, or selflessly. The chance of blessings from God increases manifold this way as compared to them who pray only for themselves.

In the previous chapter, we have seen that the shopkeeper helped the roadside beggar. While drinking water out of extreme thirst, he made millions of sincere prayers to God from his heart for the shopkeeper. Each relaxing drop of water which was being drunk was the prayer for goodness of the shopkeeper directly or indirectly from the heart of the beggar.

So, to get more and more blessings from God, the only way is to help others sincerely without any expectations. Let others pray for us. God will surely hear others prayer for us. Don't forget that when your mind is filled with more and more love, you can proudly claim that you are having God in your subconscious mind in the form of Love.

But still there are so many other instances that come in life when self-prayer is necessary. For example, while going through an examination, starting a new business, constructing a new house etc. But what is the significance of these self-prayers to God. Here we pray to get a positive move. Just as we take permission of our parents before we go somewhere, we seek permission of God for creating a divine atmosphere to start a new thing of whatever nature to achieve success.

A question may arise in your mind about the surety of prayer by all those who we have helped. Obviously all may not be doing so. But while helping others, we have already generated good karma for us and that will surely revert with good health, wealth, prosperity and peace in our life as per the theory "for every action there is an equal and opposite reaction"

Chapter 6

Incentive from God

I have interacted with many of my friends who have a lot of faith in God, do regular prayers and often visit temples. They also hold a respectable position in their job and earn a handsome salary ranging from 20 K to 40 K. They lead a tension free, healthy and settled life. But everyone wishes to get an extra income apart from their regular income to make their dreams come true. With their salary, they can manage their bare essentials like food, schooling for children and other minor incidental expenses.

Let me start with example of one of my friends, one among them had been working in a media company as a Chief Reporter for the last 14 years and he is leading a normal life with the salary that he is drawing. We can call him JN. I assume that he will be earning around Rs. 30 K per month. I met him approximately 4 years ago in my office. He came to me to share some of his plans as he wanted to do something extra apart from his job. His plan was related to journalism like making a news site on the net. He was expecting my help in this to develop a website for him and to plan and manage his news site. He was reluctant to leave his job till his news site grew to a higher level and gave him decent income.

So I approached a software professional asking for a quotation for the development of the news site. The amount quoted was too high for JN to bear. A good website forms the base of a news site. In order to get his work economically expedited, JN approached one of his friends working for a government IT company. Fortunately, JN's friend did not charge him anything. But when we go for a free service, definitely the energy level of the work we are planning goes down. The outcome did not come in good shape as we could pressurize or direct the IT personnel to develop the site as we desired.

If we want to compete or standout compared to other news sites, the quality of the site had of paramount importance.

Hence we had to rework on our site which took us 4 to 6 months to finalize, yet the quality was not up to the mark and we could not refer to anybody.

Anyway, I did not show much interest to work on that website because of its average quality. My friend, JN was trying to run it through some of his other friends. Unfortunately, he couldn't generate the desired traffic. Google didn't accept this site for placing advertisements for monetary benefit, even after one year.

In the meanwhile, he was always pressurizing me to join hands with him and lead this as a prime media company luring me on account of name, fame and prosperity. After a few months, the site was put on hold without putting any updates on it. Even others who were updating it stopped continuing with the site.

But his dream of running such a site still persisted. However, I maintained a healthy relationship with him because he has always helped me a lot. Whenever, I have to get something published, it is done through his media company where he works. In my mind I had an intention to help him properly to continue his dream project by investing my money and brain in it. Initially when he had approached me, I was also facing teething troubles in my business.

Whenever he comes to Varanasi (as his workplace is in the next district which is about 100 km away from my city), he visits the important temples along with me. He prays very sincerely and with dedication.

Even though, he is such a dedicated worshipper of God, but for the last 14 years, the company has not promoted him or raised his salary to the extend he deserve. Notably the company will not promote him to a higher position or raise his salary because of his dedication and sincerity while praying.

His life went on normally because he had faith in God and he is a good human being by nature. His family was happy, kids were going to school and living in a normal middle-class life style.

But in order to get an out of turn promotion or getting an incentive from the company he will have to do something extra for the company. Many companies have incentive schemes for their employees, especially if they perform well for the growth of the company. Even some time one can expect out of turn promotion too. It depends on what extra and extraordinary work or contribution you make for the company.

In the same way, let's apply this scheme for our life also. If you have a dream to grow, either to get a promotion or to do well in a business, you have to do something extra. In one's life, there is nobody to boss, nobody to give you promotion or growth. But here the Boss is GOD. If you give extra, you will get it back immediately, that's the law of nature. If you are taking something from God or Nature, you have to reciprocate or return it immediately. Even the breathe you inhale, you cannot hold it within you for more than 15 seconds, you have to expel Carbon-dioxide in return within 15 seconds. So the give and take process is an important aspect of life.

All creatures whether big or small belong to this unique creation of God – the World. Fortunately we human beings are endowed with an extra ordinary faculty of reasoning which has immense potential. What is desired is to apply it in a justified manner. It is well known to everybody that the universe abounds in natural resources meant for all. All have equal right to harness the natural wealth to their level of satisfaction. But we have to do something extra in the form of good deeds to reap its benefits in the best possible manner.

Let's us revert to JN's matter.

He has an intense desire to grow in stature and improve his economic status.

I have had a interview with him. Here is a short excerpt from the conversation that I had with him.

Me: What is your age?

JN: 44 years

Me: What is your salary?

JN: Around 25 K

Me: How many years have you been working for?

JN: 14 years

Me: Have you read some useful books in 14 years on different subject ?

JN: "Yes, very few."

Me: Have you tried to learn something apart from journalism in the past couple of years?

JN: No.

Me: What extra input have you given to wish for extra in life?

JN: Nothing, only prayers.

The excuses given by JN were: over time spent in the office, extreme job tension due to time bound work and tedious work which leaves him with almost no time to think about him.

I counter questioned him "If you have no time for self improvement and working on yourself worth, where is God at fault?"

JN was quiet, unable to say anything. He realized his fault and make up his mind to work upon his grey areas.

One fine day, because of a promotion issue or a tussle with a colleague in the office, he left his job. But the next day he started worrying. It would at-least three months to stand in any other field, then how he could manage his family expenses for these three months.

It was surprising to learn that the man who wished to start a news site and expected bigger things in life, working for 14 long years, saved nothing to survive even for three months, leave apart having a big, fat saving to invest in a business or so.

Undoubtedly, he is an experienced fellow but there were two others whose promotion was due. According to JN, they didn't deserve the promotion. JN felt that he had richer experience and optimistic attitude towards his job. But a dilemma that lingered in his mind was that one of his colleagues was in the good books by his boss owing to his sycophancy.

Whatever the case may be, whether he is experienced or not, having a good attitude or bad, that did not matter at all. The other person who is in the line for promotion is also a human being like us. He too has a family and kids, and wants to fulfill many desires in life. He and his family will also be happy when he got promoted.

Here we have a lesson to learn. We all fall in the same line and that is why we are not growing. It's because of our thought process which does not let us grow.

Therefore, we should cleanse our mind of negativities and wish the best for everybody.

This attitudinal shift allows us to grow into better human beings.

Let me give you another example for better understanding of the above mentioned thought.

There is a person called "RAM"

He is a diligent man and has a sound qualification. Currently he is working as a clerk in a government office (say 40% growth level). With continues professional development (CPD) and positive attitude towards work, he can leverage his efficiency multiple times (say he can reach upto 100%). This is the utmost that he can achieve in his life time.

An example:

Clerk's Actual Growth & Standard Level is__________40%.

With false ego and wrong attitude________________100%.

(without actually achieved, means he lost his 60% more actual growth by filling it with false ego, so now no space for further development).

But if

Actual Growth & Standard Level is _______________40%.

By his humbleness and attitude he is at ________20%.

Means 20% more he has reserved or generated, and apart from that additional 60% is still there.

So with good attitude he will grow

40% + 20% + 60% =120%.

Because of his super-inflated ego instead of being here at 40% he is behaving like he is at the top (100%). This implies that if he goes by his mind and ego he is at 100%, sitting at the top with his false ego. He has filled up all his space for growth with his ego, without even actually reaching there. He could have attained a decent and respectable growth by being laborious by improving his educational qualification and by gaining rich experience of work.

Contrary to this if he would have been simple, amicable and would have maintained a low profile, means sitting at 20% by humble attitude (actually he is at 40%), he still would have a space to grow up to 20% more from the currently actually achieved level and the extra 60% he can achieve and reach 100% growth plus 20% more.

But the problem is that without giving any input, a person starts thinking that he deserves the best, he is the best. He doesn't even venture into new arenas and at the same time he is neither creative nor innovative. If you not abreast with new knowledge and experience in different fields how can you think about achieving new goals and get success quickly indifferent fields. For that you have to bring a change in your thinking pattern. If you intend to quit your job for a new one, you have to plan in the past and save in a way that you will be able to manage the family at-least six months,

So the question now arises how can one achieve the extra incentive from God?

The answer is very simple, by doing something extra for God.

What is that extra that you do for God? "Selfless Service."

Just as it is your duty to manage your family and your office, similarly it is your duty to serve the society too. There are so many little things you can do for society. There are many poor people in the society striving for their basic needs or bare essentials. You should be thankful to God that you are leading a normal life. Even though you have no extra income or surplus arrangements for meeting your daily requirements or fulfilling your desires you are not hand to mouth also. So, you have to do your bit to help the needy people.

The universal law says 10% of your profit after all deductions is not yours. It's called Tithing. Try to distribute 10% of your income, 10% of your comfort, 10% of your happiness, 10% of your time, 10% of your health, 10% of your knowledge, 10% of your experience and 10% of whatever you are enjoying in life to those who deserve it. It is natural that you have to reciprocate what you accept. You cannot insist that you will inhale air but will not expel. You have to do that. Hence reciprocation in any form is expected of everybody.

Often we come across many situations in our life when somebody needs help. It is not necessary that it will be a financial help, but normally we turn a deaf ear to such requests. But if you are a firm believer in God, understand that God is giving you an opportunity to do something extra so that He can think about giving you extra. You may feel pleasure in spending time at the temple neglecting your duty in the form of social service, but God doesn't listen to your prayer in this form. God becomes happy when you share yourself for other's necessities.

But excuses are the main problem with people.

If you are an ardent believer of God, have confidence in God. If you decide to quit your job all of a sudden and want to concentrate on a new line of business, and at the same time you are concerned about your family, regarding the management of expenses and other important responsibilities that you are shouldering, then we can say you have no faith in Him. If you have faith, leave it to Him and go ahead with your decision.

It's our belief that we have deep faith in God, but actually No. We believe that we work and earn money, that's why we are living; we manage our family that's why they are living.

This is not true. Everything is managed by God. You cannot even imagine where you will be the very next moment? How will your life be like?

Consider the various objects of nature like animals, trees, birds, plants on earth. Are they going for any job to get their food? No. They are also a part of the universe; they are living beings like us. They too need food to survive. Do they die immediately after birth because their parents are unable to feed them or because they have no job ? But who feeds them? Interestingly, the Creator (God) feeds them. They also get their food. They also live and lead a normal life like the species of their family.

Similarly like other living beings on the earth, most of the humans too live in the world. The normal middle class families who concentrate on their job only for their livelihood, too, earn enough to manage their basic essentials.

But, we, humans have a chance to diversify our lifestyle by utilizing our faculties that we are endowed with by using our rationale, utilizing our learning and thinking capacity and doing selfless service.

So be ready to get extra incentives from God. Start doing extra for God. God is your boss. Your life will go on as it is and you will be passing each day with the same life style. But when you decide to do extra for God he will also plan extra for you.

I have heard a cliché from many talented people that "Luck never helped me." But I have a different version, "We never helped luck," we were not ready when luck was in our favour.

Again let us revert to JN's story. In the past 14 years, neither luck favoured him nor opportunity came in his way. That's true, but next morning if Luck is ready to go by his side and favour him, will he be ready with something to let the luck work on him? Has he tried something sincerely? Is he doing something extra from his side properly? Has he learned something extra? I know the answer is a big 'No.' Many people sit at home, who are very talented. They are simply wasting their talents because they do not want to do hard work. But we always say "Luck never helped him."

I have drawn the inspiration citing this anecdote from Guruji who practiced Kathak Dance. He is a teacher in a Kathak School and draws a handsome salary. But he prefers to spend more time inside the house. He often praises himself saying he is the only good dancer in the city. He never goes to see other's dance performances because he is of the opinion that all other dancers will be inferior to him. He believes in teaching only those students who pay him highly. He never participates in any programme if they do not offers him a handsome amount. He is not social either. He is a great exponent of Kathak Dance, but he is never seriously concerned in his professional growth and significance. He might have earned a good name and fame and people might have respected him a lot, but he was like the clerk as I have mentioned earlier; sitting in a false aura of 100% achievements created by his own ego, with no space to grow. In such a situation all curses and blames go in the court of luck.

So let's work together for a high incentive (blessing) from God.

Before concluding this chapter let me explain a little more about prayer.

As I have mentioned earlier, always asking for something for one self from God is a selfish act of negative nature. Wishes will not be fulfilled. But pray wisely, as I said, deal with God in a very friendly manner. If you have a sincere desire in your heart to donate Rs. 10,000 every month to a very poor school nearby, you concentrate your prayer on that. If you are sincere in your decision, pray to God to make you capable so that you can easily donate Rs. 10,000 to that school. Here you make a deal with God for donating. You asked nothing for yourself, but you prayed for something else. Ultimately you know what you have done? You have prayed to God to enhance your income level to Rs. 1 Lakh per month. How? Because you have made a promise to God for tithing here. In other words if you explain your prayer, "God please make me capable by next year to be able to pay Rs. 10,000 every month to that poor school nearby my house and it will be10% of my income." Then your income would be One Lakh. You are actually praying if my income will be Rupees One Lakh per month, I will donate Rs. 10,000. In this style pray, your selfish interest comes first.

If you want your children to do well in school, donate books and pencils to poor students, and provide/supply/donate old uniforms and books to the needy. If you want to wear good clothes, help with clothes to others. If you want to be in good health, help others who are in bad health. If you do not have enough money to donate, at-least donate your time for somebody. One can do Social Service and Charity even without spending a penny. Your time, good words, teaching all comes under charity and you will get everything back in abundance from God. God never returns you in the same proportion, rather if you do 10%, you will get 100% in return. It will also help us to neutralize some of our bad karmas.

My life experience is the out come of a few words but powerful words which were written in my mind as words on a hard rock "Vasudhaiva Kutumbakam" (*Mahopanishad* VI. 71–73) which means the world is one family. I understood that those who are concerned only with their family will not be as useful to this society as to those who are maintaining excellent relationship within the family as well as with the society, These people have positive relations extended through out the world. To them the whole world is a single unit, a single family.

Last but not the least I would like to quote from Bhagavad Gita –

"A man who sees action in inaction and inaction in action has understanding among men and discipline in all action he performs."

"The person whose mind is free from attachment, who has subdued the mind and senses, and who is free from desires, attains the supreme perfection of freedom from karma through renunciation."

Chapter 7

Karma (Actions)

Maharishi Mahesh Yogi defines Karma as "the philosophy of action." I am a true believer in Karma and therefore ditto his words. From thoughts to action, whatever we do in a day is "Karma" and Sakyong Mipham rightly confesses that Karma, like gravity is so basic, that we don't even notice it.

Problems, joys, sorrows, happiness's, success, ups and down are all the outcome of our karma (action). It is a well known fact that the result of an action depends on the way we do it. Positive action reaps positive results, negative action reaps negative results. I believe in karma strongly and I also believe firmly in the fact that if you put out positive vibes to everybody that's all you are going to get in return. You are rewarded with what you give whether good or bad. So, one's own karma is responsible to bring either happiness or sorrow in his life.

From this we conclude that karma is bi-directional. If our acts are virtuous, the seeds of our plant will yield good fruits and if our acts are full of vices, they result in nothing else but suffering and agonies. Thus, every karma done whether good or bad strikes on some chord that vibrates in eternity. Even Annie Besant is of the opinion that belief in karma ought to make the life pure, strong, serene and glad. Only our own deeds can hinder us; only our own will can fetter us. Once let me recognize this truth, and the hour of liberation has struck. Nature cannot enslave the soul that by wisdom has gained power and uses both in love.

But is it possible that all the time we done gative karma through ignorance ?

If a person has a habit of taking unlimited pegs of alcohol day in day out, it is a negative karma and he is very much aware of it. But still he continues with it. Medical Science says that alcohol kills 3 blood cells in our body and gradually it affects the functioning of liver and kidney and most of the people who take alcohol without any limitation are aware that it is harmful for them. In their consciousness, the place where the God form originates, always warns them to control their urge. They can hear the warning bell of God; every person can feel the voice of God that is why we say that the habit of taking alcohol is wrong and one should control it. But if one ignores that voice and continues to take it regularly, one has to suffer in the later stage of life.

Some people have a tendency of cheating others very easily. Even though their conscious won't allow them to do that they ignore that inner voice of God and easily cheat others.

Here I am reminded of an incident of an astrologer who visited my neighbor. He was a relative of one of my friend, Digamber. Digamber is a railway employee and he introduced this astrologer to me. As usual, we too discussed many things with the astrologer about our future etc.

He had casted a very good impression on me as he read my spiritual way of living my life. During the course of my interaction with him, I also learnt many things and I was also impressed.

One morning while he was staying in my friend's house he visited my house for tea and spent more than 15 minutes advising us on many issues. That day my friend Digamber was out of station on his official duty. While exchanging our views, the astrologer got a telephone call and after attending it he felt sad and his eyes were filled with tears. We could gauge that something untoward had happened with him and he was in deep trouble. We were panicked and enquired about the cause of his fret.

With tearful eyes he said, his son had met with a serious accident and has been admitted in the ICU. He is in a critical condition and he has to go back very soon. We too requested him to leave as soon as possible. Unfortunately there was no train that day and he could catch a train only on the next morning. He requested us to help with a huge amount so that he could manage the critical situation that he was in. He also ensured that he will return the amount as soon as he reaches there. We were speechless and without any hesitation we helped him with the required amount of money. He also requested us to arrange a morning ticket for him and that too we did. Next day in the morning, my driver dropped him at the railway station but before getting down from the car the astrologer enquired at the reservation counter because he wanted to cancel the ticket.

When we came to know about this from the driver, we immediately contacted Digamber and apprised him of whatever had happened. On his return, he called up the family of the astrologer and enquired about the well-being of his son and family. The wife of the astrologer said, they were all doing well and his son had just come back from school and no accident had taken place. The astrologer cooked up a painful story to misuse our humbleness and spirituality to earn money. With the money that he got after the cancellation of ticket, he left for another city.

The astrologer committed this crime knowing very well that he is creating a negative karma for himself, but he did not understand God and His nature, so he did it.

Whatever activity we plan to do, our mind warns us immediately whether we are going to do a negative thing or a positive thing.

Let us look at another example.

Suppose, a girl is standing on the other side of the road and is in a hurry to cross the road to come to this side. While doing that action she speaks to somebody within her. Shall I run or wait for the traffic to clear ?And when the road is cleared of traffic, she was about to run and immediately she sees that a bike is coming very fast, and she stops again because her inner conscious said that the bike can hit her if she crosses the road. But if she ignores and runs, anything can happen to her and she will be responsible for the outcome.

While doing each and every activity, the God form in our mind speaks to us. Though there is no expression on our face and our lips don't move, yet we are in constant conversation with the God.

Here I wish to revert to one more thing that relates to the astrologer and about the karma he did and we did.

If we explain the story of the astrologer about cheating us of money to any of our family members or any outsider, what will be their advice? They will say that it was a bad karma from our side. You shouldn't have given money to him.

But what happened actually here? Who did the bad karma? We, who helped him or he who cheated us?

After hearing about the critical condition of his son, the God form of our mind associated with the feeling of his agony and empathy, proceeded to help him. So what we did was a good karma from our side. We helped him, thats all. It's a good karma. I agree that some money has gone, but the same God form will be happy with our karma because it was a service and help extended to somebody in an emergency hour and in return it is God's responsibility to bring prosperity back to us. But you cannot ever see in to the future that when and in what way God returns to you something against the Good Karma you did by helping the astrologer.

The astrologer earned that money through a created story with an intention of plotting a plan of treachery. Temporarily, his wish was fulfilled but he is not aware that in future how and in what way will he be losing manifold amount of the money that he had earned through his drama.

It is clear that everywhere we need to understand God and the nature of his actions.

Let us take up another example to understand the concept of blessing or incentive from God, and how God calculates our actions.

Imagine there are three shops in a row on the road over a distance of 50 meters and it is noon time. A beggar comes towards the first shop and as soon as the shop keeper sees the beggar he takes out a coin from his money box and throws it at him even before he gets near the shop.

The beggar throws an unpleasant eye at the shop keeper for throwing the coin towards him. He takes the coin with respect and moves to the second shop. Here the beggar gets near the shop and the shopkeeper. The shop keeper was busy with his customers but he took a coin and gave it to the beggar. He then moves to the third shop. Seeing the beggar, the shop keeper scolded the beggar for wandering in the city in this extreme heat. He advised him to take rest somewhere for a few hours and start begging in the evening when this extreme heat fades out. The shop keeper offers him some water to drink and asks whether he has eaten something or not. The beggar said he already had and sat there for an hour. When he was about to go, the third shop keeper also gave him a coin of the same denomination as the other shop keepers.

I think I don't need to explain what the God form inside the beggar felt while dealing with all three shop keepers. The first one gave a coin but his attitude was totally negative. If he had rejected the beggar without a coin, it would have been better, but by throwing a coin, he did 90% bad karma and 10% good karma offering a coin. The second shop keeper was better than the first one and he might have done100% good karma. The third shop keeper also did 100% good karma too. Owing to his good karma, he will earn incentives too from God.

For every action there is an equal and opposite reaction. If not today, then sometime later it happens in front of your eyes, but it happens for sure, you might not know about it. But if you watch your life very carefully, you will experience it.

Karma as Helping Others

Life has its own way of baffling us when we feel low because of constant failures. And when we think them is fortunes are over, life treats with us another big kick, thereby letting our morale down once again.

But, it is of paramount importance to remember that setbacks, misfortune, failures and tragedies are part and parcel of our life. How we manage to find happiness in the midst of these is by and large dependent on our attitude, perseverance and will power to sail through even the toughest times without giving up. Last but not the least we must have faith in ourselves and our capabilitics as these seemingly wide area of fear, disappointment, pain and heartache which appear to engulf major part of life are just brief, insignificant moments of our life, that will certainly pass. Tough times never last; they are ephemeral.

Most of the people in their bad times have the habit of seeking help from those whom they have helped in the past. Undoubtedly, one may have helped innumerable people sincerely when he had enough wealth and was in pink spirits. But when time changes, he too needs some help to manage his life's troubles and obviously we expect it from those whom we have helped. But most of the time 99% of them donot help us in return. They might be in a good position to help and may have all the resources but they ignore the needs of others. Even though they can stand in life and achieve many things if other's help them, but their mentality has been changed when their time changes. Sadly they are reluctant to reciprocate in the same manner.

Henry Ford rightly confesses, "When everything seems to be going against you, remember that the airplane takes off against the wind, not with it."

When we face such trying situations obviously we get disappointed and we will lose faith in God. We wonder to see this kind of attitude from people and probably we feel like we did a wrong thing by helping others, because they do not help us in return when we need their help.

But in fact, we are wrong. Our thinking that we helped them is wrong. We cannot help anybody and we have not helped either. Remember prosperity helps in making friends and adversity helps in trying them. Every trouble, every misfortune and every failure carries with it the seed of an equivalent or higher value.

Let us think in a different way, we helped God, and others got the help from God. As I have mentioned in the earlier chapters, God that originated in our heart ultimately helped others like the shop keeper helped the road side beggar.

So rather than expecting help in return from those, whom you have helped, seek help from God. Remember, God will not forsake you. The agonies and afflictions in life are orchestrated by God, out of his affection for us.

I have always believed in the age old adage that God helps those who help themselves. Those who have faith in God, pray to him during the time of crisis asking God to help them out of that current situation.

Put your trust in God, God will come to your help also, yes of course in different ways as we have seen in earlier chapters, may be in the form of humans, but they may not be those whom you have already helped. The helping person will probably be unknown to you, or he may be a friend of yours whom you have never helped or you never expected that he would help you.

Because when you had helped God, the God form of Love originated in your heart, and that Love form of God forced you to help others and now for you also the Love form of God will come to help. You just have to wait and see in what way it comes. It's up to God only.

This is my experience in life.

Many people come to me with a complaint about God that they are not rich notwithstanding their spiritual and having extreme faith in God. They have not committed any crime or wrong doing in their life but still they are not rich, but happily living a normal life without any risk. They have the helping mentality too and they are living with positive action and attitude. But there are many people in the society who have no faith in God, even commit many crimes, and do so many bad things in life with man power and money power. We can say they are negative people with negative attitudes. But they are rich with loads of money. However, the positive people sometimes confuse seeing immense wealth with people with negative attitudes.

But if you just forget that richness, money power and man power and think from God's perspective, you will feel richer than those negative people. How? People with positive thought, positive action and with positive attitude with faith in God have a good heart from where the Love form of God originates. Your richness is your heart from where the Love form of God originates within you. But this won't be happening in people with negative attitudes. If you think this way, you will fell yourself rich always. But if you count the richness with material things, you will feel poor always.

Helping and punishing all depends on karma (positive and negative doings of life) and the authority who decides and manages is God.

But if the God form originates in your heart, be happy with that. You are the richest person having such a great place in your body.

Chapter 8

Beauty of God

A new born baby is a living proof of the significance of life. Its innocence, fragility, agility and beauty wins the heart of everyone. It is a beautiful miracle of God and an example of his unique creation. When we see a child, it can immediately put a smile on our face because what we see and experience in our mind is the beauty of God. Beauty and talent exist everywhere in the universe. They are beyond any explanation.

As a child grows up, either the child or his parents can identify the talent within him and if the talent is nurtured well, the child can become a master of that art. Various forms of art like dancing, singing, photography, engineering, painting, learning, reading, writing, serving others etc. help one create his identity and carve a niche for himself. Some doubt may arise regarding how learning, teaching, serving etc. can be called an art form.

Whatever be the nature of an action, when it is done with love and perfection, it becomes and art. It's the perfection that is art, which is attained because of your passion and affection for that particular action. Hence, when such an art or talent is performed in front of the public, the performance wins the heart of the audience watching it. They appreciate the artist heartily which implies the art performed has perfection of some higher degree.

Now let's take an example of an artist who draws pictures and paintings. Though an artist paints a picture, the real artist is not him but God because the art form of God from in his heart gives birth to a beautiful painting. No person can become an artist in any form of art until and unless he carries the art form of God within him from birth.

Let's take an example of things that happen around us. Visit a nearby college or university of performing arts or visual arts and we can see many students who have decided to learn a particular art of their choice.

It is noteworthy that there are two categories of students. One who want to get a degree for namesake and the other one wants to nurture his/her talent apart from getting a degree. The latter ones are called real artists, in true sense.

The second category of students work day and night to achieve perfection in their area of interest. Wherever and whenever they get a chance to perform their art, they always stand in the forefront to give their best without any expectation. They attend and participate in such programmes to nurture and enhance their talent and do it with full devotion to create an excellent form of art that is par excellence.

A similar attitude can be seen in the teachers and professors also. The real artists who have love for their art will create more and more art forms and will continuously work on improvisation, nurturing their talent day by day and sharing it with their students. They are not attending the college because they are teachers or professors. They are there because they love their art. Salary or remuneration is secondary for them. Their main focus is on creating the art form which originates in their heart as an art form of God.

I have seen in many higher education institutions that many talented artists spend time just to cover up their duty time. They neither make effort to nurture the art nor show their contribution by creating some wonderful art form to the world.

But those who understand the value of the art form of God within them; they will do wonderful creations with their art and become maestros.

So, the art or talent we see in a person is the art or talent form of God and what we experience while seeing it is the beauty of God. Both the art forms of God and the beauty of art are invisible. We simply experience and feel the pleasure derived from it.

Whoever is an artist whether a singer, dancer, player, or any other, whatever talent or art reflects in his life is art form of God and what forces us to appreciate the art and the artist is the beauty of God.

If we observe every person closely, we will find that we are all carrying some talent within us. If we properly understand, nurture and develop it, then we can be the master of that talent and that will give us success in our lives.

The various objects of nature that we see around us every time gives us a strong concept of the glory and magnanimity of God. The universe testifies that this omnipotent power with His infinite faculties, extraordinary goodness, created the earth and filled it with vivaciousness, beauty and happiness. Even in their most blighted time, all objects reveal the par excellent talent of the Supreme Power. Wherever, we may go, we find His imprints and His goodness. All the beauty and brightness that adorn the earth, speak volumes about God and His ingenuity.

Take a look at your surroundings, the vast universe, the sky, floating clouds, the moon, innumerable stars, animals and birds, scenic beauty- all these creations leaves us mesmerized and enraptured.

In the earth, sea and sky, with their beautiful hues and shades, mixed and blended in perfect harmony, we see His glorious creations. – Marvelous mountains, ceaseless ocean, ever-flowing rivers, tall trees, the rising and setting sun all point to His art creation and tell of his care even for the humblest of His creatures. They are the living beauties of nature and God's gift to mankind.

Many of us might have seen a shadow of ours or any other item. Intriguing is the fact that who creates that shadow? And If you carefully watch the shadow, you can visualize an art in it. The shadow is created when something blocks the light's path, and what is blocked becomes a shadow and ultimately it's an art. When we appreciate a particular shadow seeing its perfection, we can say, it is the beauty of God.

If we look at the sky, we often see the birds fly together forming a design and sometimes they play in the air like the military helicopters performing their air performance. It's the talent and beauty of God. We humans get training in college to nurture our talent, but other living and non-living beings perform automatically with the art and talent form of God they have been endowed with.

The science proves that the cosmic energy contains seven colours, and which we can see with our eyes while passing the light through a prism. The rainbow seen during rainy season is an another example of colours in spectrum.

Albert Einstein in a letter to his friend referred to the universe as "a miracle or an eternal mystery….which reinforced as our knowledge expands." Since the inception of civilization, man has been trying to comprehend the working and mind of the engineer behind such enchanting creations.

At an even more fundamental level, the basic conditions necessary for the emergence and sustenance of life appear to have been engineered by God or what Stephen Hawkings admits, "except as the act of a God who intended to create being like us."

It is now evident that the first engineer is no doubt, God? If today there is an engineer who develops a car, tv, fridge oreven arobot, he learns it from the engineering of God within our body. Such unlimited things are there in nature that exist as the art and beauty of God. If we watch it carefully, we can realize the perfection of God's art and creation.

There are three main tenets of the faith in God; one is that God is seen in all the natural creations, the second one is that all faiths and religions have easy accessibility to the Divine Truth and the third one is that the babies are born with a part of divinity.

A sound knowledge of the omnipotence of God is the foundation of all kinds of education and service that we render to the society. It is this knowledge that can make us like God in character, beauty and talent.

Chapter 9

Religion

Religions and belief rest upon ethical principles of equality, love, kindness, sympathy and to meet human needs in broad sense. The precept that Love and treat equally one and all is part of religion. The same belief permeates in all religions. While most of religions are ingrained with sense of oneness, history probably bears a record of more examples of inhumanity. Let us consider the instance of our natural resources. Are they stratified for a particular religion, community or sect? Definitely No.

Equality is imperative for achievement of satisfaction and progress of everybody. Yet discrimination is pervasive in every nook and corner of the globe, in all the strata of society and manifests in various forms.

Each and everyone on this earth have the liberty and right to use whatever is available in the universe. Whether it is a sentient being or non-sentient being, all belong to this universe.

All religions and discriminations are constructed by man himself for example there are many political parties in a particular country. Every party has a name, a leader and sub-leaders and its followers. Each party has its own ethics, has a different flag, different symbols, different motto, but they all belong to one country and are equal.

If a man has five sons and if the code of conduct and life ethics of all five sons are different, it doesn't mean that their parents are different. Obviously, the characters of all five sons may be different, but they all belong to same parents. Being a parent, their love and care will be equal for all sons, because all five sons belong to them.

My simple conviction is that religion does not recognize differentiation on the basis of gender, caste, tribes or background. The idea of equality of all persons is recognized in human religion which everyone should abide by.

Chapter 10

Spirituality

In broad sense, spirituality refers to any praxis of reformation of oneself in line with traditional and religious ideals. But it has different implications too. For some, it implies an active participation in religious activities while for others it's yoga, meditation, deep reflection, etc. In other words, it is medium of seeking solace and peace in life.

It's a human nature to have affection for things or be devoted to certain things in life fully. Normally one is called SPIRITUAL if he is engaged in some religious activity or showing some devotion to God in one form or the other. People who visit various places of worship, or places where some activities related to God are organized from time to time consider themselves to be spiritual.

Is this actually called spirituality? I don't know. But what I have understood about spirituality is different.

According to me, spirituality is the stage of realizing self and the other self as equal. It is a great way of gaining perspective, recognizing that our role in life has more importance than what we do every day. One of the important benefits of spirituality is that it reaffirms and realigns your sense of self to something you may not have imagined ever existed within you. This knowledge helps you to broaden your horizon, makes you feel important and esteemed and helps you to find that divine light that exists inside of you. This light is present in every person who is born in this world.

If a God believing person has a deep rooted belief that he belongs to a superior religion and he accepts and rejects people in the society according to their religion or community status, how can he be spiritual? As we have learned from the previous chapters, the God form originates in a clear heart.

Spirituality connects you with the very powerful and divine force that exists everywhere in the universe and knits it into a unified whole. It is a well established fact that nothing can mobilize you to accomplish your targets and provide you with an effective solution. It is only spiritual knowledge that helps you in going a long way.

I had a heart touching experience recently in my life. Let me admit 50% of this story is true but 50% I have created and continued to show the end result. The climax that I have created to show is that all the karmas will be reciprocated in the future as per the universal rule “every action has an equal and opposite reaction.” Very often we are unaware of it, as we cannot connect with a good thing that has happened to us, with a good karma we did in the past.

A few years ago, I went to stay at a friend’s house for one month for the purpose of doing some study. He lived with his family. As I was very close, I often visited him. One day, his wife, Lalita, who works as a Staff Nurse in the Medical College, was discussing a small incident that had happened in her hospital very enthusiastically.

Ramanand, I guess, was the name of a peon cum sweeper of the section where she was working. The main duty of Ramanand was to keep the duty room clean and other surrounding areas. He belonged to the lower strata of the society. The marriage of his daughter was fixed and he was excited and happy about it. The same day, he visited the duty in charge of his section, who comes from a higher community. She is a blind believer of God and also regularly performs many devotional rituals too. Ramanand handed over the marriage invitation card to her and other staff in the duty room including Lalita, my friend's wife. His invitation card for all other people of his community was of normal quality; which reflected his status in the society. But especially for these nursing staff, he had bought some expensive and attractive invitation cards. Hehanded over the card to all of them with a humble request that they should all visit the marriage function of his daughter.

As soon as he left the room, the duty in charge collected the invitation cards from all the other staff and threw them into the dustbin. She shouted and said, "How dare he invite us to the marriage of his daughter? Doesn't he know his status? He should at least think about his profession. How could he expect that we, who belong to a higher class, will visit his place? How could'n he forget that he is a sweeper or cleaner here"? She warned her colleagues that if any of them attends the marriage of his daughter, she will transfer him/her from the department to another department.

Going by the warning of the duty in charge they all decided not to attend the marriage of Ramanand's daughter. Instead they will send another peon with 1000 Rupees as contribution on behalf of all of them. So she collected the sum of 1000 Rupees from all the nurses and handed it over to another peon. She advised the peon to attend the marriage function and handover the amount as a gift and token on their behalf. He was strictly instructed to return without even taking a glass of water if offered.

So, Lalita was narrating this episode in the afternoon on the day of the marriage function. The marriage function was supposed to be held at night.

I asked my friend and his wife Lalita to accompany me to that marriage function in the evening. But she refused to go saying that her duty in charge will shift her from the current section of her duty. I insisted and convinced them to go with an assurance from my end that nothing will happen in her duty room and even if anything goes wrong, I will manage it by complaining to the higher authorities. I also requested Lalita to call the peon who was supposed to carry 1000 Rupees as a token to accompany us to Ramanand's place.

As told, the peon reached our place and we were all ready by 7 pm to attend that function. We went in the optra car and I took the onus of driving. Very soon we reached the marriage venue but a little early, so went to his home which was close by.

Ramanand was standing a little far from us and was gaping at us. As per his belief people with such a big car were not expected there. Even though he had given the invitation card to everybody in the duty room including the duty in charge, he was rest assured that nobody would come to the marriage because he belonged to lower community in the society. But for the sake of satisfaction and worldliness, he had distributed the card.

We were constantly watching him. He was busy making final arrangements for the guests. In between, he looked at us many times, wondering about our identity. As we did not come out of our car, he could not control his inquisitiveness and came near the driver seat to clarify our identity. As I was the driver, we were unknown to each other. He could not make out who all had come for the wedding or was it a case of mistaken identity? A little later, he asked me where I wanted to go as he had not seen us before. So I hinted him to look behind me. He immediately turned towards the mand was shocked.

"Oh! Sister" he exclaimed shockingly.

His face lit up with joy and it was like he was looking at one of the seven wonders of the world. He was on cloud nine.

He said, "Sister…you are here…for this marriage function. I am so fortunate."

Lalita nodded in affirmation.

He then, opened the door and requested her to come out as if he was welcoming a celebrity. We too joined them. He ran to open the entrance of his small house and told the other people in his home that sister and her family have come from the hospital to grace the occasion of my daughter's marriage. His happiness was inexpressible. He forgot for a moment that it was the marriage of his daughter. But he was so elated that a family from a higher strata visited his house to attend the marriage. His eyes were filled with tears of happiness. He started running here and there to bring some chairs, dusted them well and requested us to be seated. He tried his best to make us feel at home. We were pleased by the way he welcomed us.

All of us felt very comfortable but sister Lalita was a little uncomfortable because of two reasons. One he was from a lower community and the second thing was the warning of her duty in charge. He introduced the members of his family to us. They offered some sweets and water. I picked up one sweet and asked him to name the shop from where he had bought the sweet. Surprisingly it was the same shop from where we too buy sweets for our home. I asked this question purposely, because I knew if he says that the sweet is made at his home, Lalita would not have taken it.

So, I told Lalita that, this sweet is from the same shop where we also buy sweets. So she can assuredly have sweets and the water, since water is an element of nature, and is not produced by Ramanand.

I told her to imagine that she is sitting in a restaurant and waiting for the sumptuous meal to be served to her. The irony of the situation is that she is absolutely unaware of the person who is cooking in the kitchen and how is the food being cooked. So, what is the point of making such a fuss? At least we should acknowledge the warmth of the person who is offering us rather than beating our brains after petty issues.

A little half-heartedly she realized the harsh truth and took the sweets and water. My friend and I happily accepted everything he offered as if we also belonged to his own community. But his biggest happiness today was not his daughter's marriage but the fact that people from a higher community visited him and honoured his invitation. He spoke about us to all his friends, relatives and guests or whosoever came to attend the marriage function and all were watching us in wonder. He was held in high esteem and earned great reputation from the members of his community. People of his community started respecting him very much. He was continuously attending us to ensure that we are comfortable and entertained properly.

Later I asked him to continue with his arrangements and finish up the last minute jobs. We assured him that we will stay there for an hour to attend the marriage. The peon was also there with us. We happily attended his marriage function and returned only after taking dinner.

After returning, I asked Lalita to express her feeling of this visit. She agreed that everything was good and she too felt comfortable, but she was afraid to think about her duty the next day. A thought that was continuously pestering her mind was what will be the repercussion of her visit to Ramanand's place when she joins her duty. I told her to have confidence and say it was your husband and a very close friend of your husband who was fortunately putting up at your house that day, who forced you to attend the marriage and you had to agree, though half-heartedly.

This is just an imagination about the way the world reciprocates the action of rejecting a person of a lower community.

We are all slave of our emotions. This expression stands true for duty in-charge. As usual Lalita attended her duty the next day. As was anticipated, the duty in charge turned a deaf ear to everything and remained angry for the whole day. We all know that when anger overpowers somebody, it makes him irrational and aggressive. The main problem is that in the fit of anger, the person denies to listen to anybody, destroys ones peace of mind and often makes great mistakes. This is what exactly happened with the duty in charge. She was burning with anger without realizing anything she exploded on all her sub-ordinates even on petty issues.

Anyway, this lingered on for a month until the day came when there was a farewell party of a senior staff member of that department who was retiring from his job.

"For every action there is an equal and opposite reaction" is one of the basic axioms of elementary physics. This stands for duty in charge here.

The party started in the evening. The guests had started arriving. My friend and I dropped Lalita to the venue. After sometime, when we went to pick her up, to our utter surprise, we came to know that the five year old son of the duty in charge who was playing with friends had fell in the septic tank. A huge crowd had gathered there and the duty in charge was weeping badly. We both rushed to that place and Lalita came running to us and said that the lady who is crying is the duty in charge who had created scene by asking us not to attend the marriage function of Ramanand's daughter who was of a lower community.

The tank was 10 feet deep and everybody was worried about the well-being of the boy.

I wandered here and there to find Ramanand. He was not there, and then I called out "Ramanand" at the top of my voice. Immediately he came and asked, "What happened sir?" I just hinted him towards the scene with my facial expression.

Without giving a second thought, he quickly jumped into the septic tank and brought the boy out of it. The boy looked so dirty that even his mother hesitated in touching him. It was Ramanand who immediately took him to the hand pump nearby and washed him thoroughly. Ramanand's shirts and slippers were so badly soiled that he decided to throw them away.

He then washed himself and brought the boy back to his mother. Now she caressed and cajoled her son with affection and love and drew him towards her heart and was looking to Ramanand with sense of gratitude.

I decided to say a few words to her and forward but Lalita and her husband stopped me. But I didn't listen and went to the duty in charge and asked her. "Would you like to carry your son with you or leave him here now?"

She was surprised to hear that. She asked me who I was and why was asking her such a question.

I said, "actually Ramanand belongs to a lower community because of which you had put an objection and warned everybody not to go to attend his daughter's marriage. Despite your warning, we attended the marriage. We are sorry and disappointed to learn that our move made you angry. Hence you became self-centered. Whenever you get angry, you say some very painful, pinching remarks to your colleagues and sub-ordinates. In fact, you seems to have little regard for those around you just because your ego is hurt."

"But now here the situation is different."

Very calmly, I told her to imagine the following situation.

"When your son fell down in the septic tank and who dared to enter that tank and save your son? Showing exemplary courage and presence of mind, the man none other than Ramanand took a plunge into the septic tank to rescue your son. This act of Ramanand won every ones heart today but for you Ramanand comes from a different social background. As he belongs to the lowest rung of the society you have no respect for him and his community. He belongs to the marginalized section and that is why his fate is to face discrimination, economic deprivation and ridicule. But if he hadn't dared to venture into this act, it would have been difficult for you to save your son. You have no respect for him and his community. He actually touched your son and washed him well. Is your son dirty by his touch now? Will you abandon him as he has been touched by a social outcaste? Despite the barriers of caste, the rigidity and narrow-mindedness, he came forward to your help."

Me continued…

"Your son has become dirty in two ways. First, as he fell into the septic tank and secondly because he was saved by a person from lower community. According to your nature, as I know, you should give up your son. If Ramanand had not been here, you would not have probably bothered to get your son out. You neither have the courage to jump into the tank nor the desire to touch him in this mess.

When such a situation arises, what will the egoistic person belonging to a higher community do? They have nothing else but to compromise.

See, how your own fundamentals are tainted by reality and if you don't compromise, you may suffer. One has to accept the reality. One has to accept the self and the other self on equal terms. This means you have to show true spirituality."

All of us have a similar basic understanding about what is right and what is wrong. The consciousness within all of us is the same. There is no higher community and lower community classification for consciousness. Remember the inflictions caused by racial injustice and discrimination are indelible and are never healed. Therefore, we must learn to have mutual understanding and respect for one another. We are all equal in the eyes of God and His love is unconditional. It is given to everyone liberally. Nature or the Universe has never classified its resources on the basis of caste, creed, race etc.

Spirituality requires the dissolving of man-made caste boundaries and discrimination. Hence the notion of equality refers to discarding any injustice and unfairness to all living beings.

One is not considered to be spiritual when he prays to God, or goes to the temple or church or mosque or any such religious places. Having devotion to God cannot be called as a state of spirituality.

Accept and embrace everybody by heart. Treat everyone kindly. Consider all belonging to one community on companionate and humanitarian grounds. Hate no one. Everyone needs love and everyone deserves it. Deep down the core, every man has a good heart, seek to understand and love everyone.

Greedy people in good times think that they are superior to others either by religion, by money or by designation or status. When they all are burnt in a crematorium after death, one is left with just 58 grams of ash. Nothing more than that because 70% of our body is water.

I will conclude this chapter with Geroge Mason's words who has very aptly remarked, "We came equals into the world, and equal shall we go out of it."

Chapter 11

Atheist & Theist

Why there are God believing people (Theist) and non-God believing people (Atheist)?. Why there are so many arguments on this subject?. If man prays and believes in God, everything in the future happens according to his wish, one will continue to believe in God. If something contrary occurs, man will be unhappy with God and later sometime he might become an atheist.

A person who is rich or is born with a silver spoon won't believe in the existence of such a God form. He behave like a King as I mentioned in earlier chapter such a man feels that everything happens according to his wish because he has enough money, comforts and man power. But he forgets that the universe and other natural phenomena are not governed by human beings. The reigns of these lies in the hands of Supreme Being.

A person as an atheist will no longer exist after he recognizes the consciousness within him or the God form within him. Suppose a father has a wish to see his son to become doctor, he coaxes him right from his childhood he has been preparing him for that. He earnestly prays to God for him. After a certain stage, the parent realizes that his son would rather like to become a management professional instead of becoming a doctor. This may lead to a change in the attitude of the parent as far as his belief in God is concerned.

I know several atheists. In my opinion they are atheist, but actually they arc the real believers of God. According to them, "Nature" or the "Universe" is God. But they do not believe in the photo or the idol form of God. They do not commit a crime and believe that as long as one follows the positive ethics of life there is no need to have blind belief in God. They ridicule a person who goes to the temple, and worships God in different forms.

The photos, statues, religion and myths are all symbolic of God's omnipresence. When we understand the real form of God, we can manifest his other forms too. To cleanse our mind, we should concentrate on prayers, confine all thoughts to our heart and develop the Love form of God within us. Seeing a photo of any God anywhere whether we believe or not, going to a temple, church or mosque even if we do believe in Him, installs some kind of positive energy within us. Even an atheist will not misbehave when he is in such a place which he may have visited for any other purpose other than spiritual practice or worshipping.

Till now, I have been expressing my own thoughts about my understanding of God.

But from now onwards I am going to share some of my own real life experiences when I actually experienced and met God. These incidents actually made me understand and visualize the form of God. What I understand and what I want to make you understand from these incidents is the outcome of the previous chapters.

The stories will enable me to explain how God is paving the way for us to experience new things in life.

✦ ✦ ✦

My Meetings with God

Before delving into the incidents, let me briefly mention few things.

One of my biggest dreams came true on 6th August 2014 when I had written the first draft of my book, "The Moments When I Met God." The book deals with spreading the message of personal development through my own real life experiences. It focuses on how to expand the way you think of yourself and the world around you. This book will empower you to think and discover the various forms of God and will help you become more valuable virtually in every phase of your life.

I started writing this book on 14th May 2007. Half of the book was written in a short time. Surprisingly, it took me more than seven years to finish the rest of the book. I believe it was God's wish that gave me positive energy and driving force to write this book. A lot of things go into writing of a book, like developing a storyline, planning out the chapterization, then the content and finally the chapters. Again I firmly affirm that finishing this book was God's plan. Today when I mull over the past time, I realize that the time was not ripe to finish the book seven years ago. I had to go through various other experiences too. So, for me, to achieve maturity, God gave me a gap of seven years. But what motivated me to finish this book? What God form worked on me to finish this book so quickly the second time, all that I have mentioned in my last chapter.

It was in 1994, in Varanasi (a district in the State of Uttar Pradesh, India) I started working in a private company as a Steno-Typist on a salary of Rs. 800 per month. I had to cover a distance of 10 km to reach my office. I got Rs. 750 or so after deductions because of late coming or taking a day off without permission. Then after one year I got an increment of Rs. 80, but I decided to leave the job for a better one. I joined an Electric Fan Manufacturing company where my salary was Rs. 1700 per month. After working for a year there, I had to go to Kerala, my native place, for my tonsil operation and I stayed there for six months. During those 6 months, I was penniless. My parents never bothered to give me any pocket money even for my bare necessities. They were so strict about money matters and they insisted that I should earn my own money and then spend. So, to meet some of my own expenses, I worked as an assistant under a construction contractor who paid me Rs. 100 per day. I got that job for 5 days only and earned Rs. 500, even then I was very happy.

After six months I came back to my work place Varanasi and joined in an export company as a stenographer again with the help of Mr. P.C. Jose, the Manager of the company. My salary was Rs. 2300 and next year I got an increment of Rs. 500. Now my salary was Rs. 2800. All other staff members got Rs. 300 as increment, but because of my efficiency I got Rs. 200 more.

From that time onwards, I started thinking how will I manage with such a meager amount? Where will my future stand? Will I be in a position to fulfill my family's need? What will be my future even if I get an increment of Rs. 300, 500 or maximum 1000 every year? This way life will continue and I will always remain hand to mouth. I was always at loggerheads with these thoughts.

I knew in the hearts of my heart that I was not wired for 2×2=4. I had to think out of the box. I started thinking on it with renewed energy. I truly believe that I have the will to succeed. Here I subscribe to Rick Pitino's views, a coach of University of Kentucky basket ball team, who said: "I am not one of those guys who believes that the key to winning is the will to win. The will to win isn't worth a nickel unless you have the will to prepare."

Like any other normal human being, I am also ambitious. Me too want to enjoy the luxuries of life. If this salary scale and increment schedule continues, probably I can change my life from a cycle to bike? Even if I change my current job and get a government job, nothing is going to change. Luckily I got a government job in Banaras Hindu University but after working for two months, I left that job and came back to the export company. Rather than continuing a normal life as a government employee I preferred to learn how to do business for a better future.

There is one more incident that motivated me to think differently when I was in Kerala for six months for my operation. My grandmother never used slippers in her life. When I asked her the reason she said that she had never worn them in her life because of not having enough money to feed her children, including my mother and other siblings. She said, for her children's sake she compromised not only with slipper but also with so many other important things in life. Then I asked her, whether her children could lead a better life than her, for which she had sacrificed so much. She became emotional, heavy hearted and with tear filled eyes, she gave an answer that was 'no.' I saw that my parents had also sacrificed a lot. I too should sacrifice for the betterment of my kids. So, who will be living without sacrifice, fulfilling all their wishes? In fact nobody will be able to do so. So at that time I decided, I will live and fulfill my wishes and will not make sacrifice to meet them.

For that higher education, higher income is necessary. If wc just live with a normal job whether government or private, we can just fulfill our basic needs, nothing else. We cannot even think of giving higher education to our children.

So, after leaving the Government job, I rejoined the export company with the intention to learn the world of business. I learned so many things from there and left the job after a year in 1998. One thing I could gather that that nobody becomes rich in a year and not everybody is born rich. But If I try, something will happen and I believed that success or failure is not an accident. It does not come to us overnight; It only knocks your door when you are ready to take risk on something. At that time, I had not even read any motivational book or attended any such seminars. I only followed my inner voice. Struggle and hurdles always obstructed my path, but I succeeded because it was the plan of God.

But there are so many people who motivated me to start my own business because they had confidence in my efficiency. I agree, it was a risky game having nothing in pocket and dreaming about starting an export business. So I decided to start with nothing. From this point onwards I started approaching life with an 'I Can' optimistic attitude, instead of 'I Can't' pessimistic attitude. Here I am reminded of a very famous quote which has won world wide acclaim also: "You don't drown by falling in the water. You drown by staying there."

✦ ✦ ✦

Now God started entering into my life in many forms.

From here onwards I started experiencing God in my real life as I had realized and understood the God form through my past experiences.

Chapter 12

Public Call Office

All through our life, we will come across different cross-sections of people. Some of them will be very influential and impressive. Babu Sahab (Anand Singh) is such a personality who is the owner of a Public Call Office(PCO). I have always regarded him as my ideal because he is aligned in every aspect: spiritual, soulful and social.

I used to visit his PCO every evening to make phone calls. His shop was about a kilometer away from my house. His attitude was very caring and I also used to share my feelings about my job, business, etc. with him. He often elevated my confidence and told me that I have the efficiency and capability to run my own business. Whenever I went there, he used to motivate me and give me a credit facility to pay in installments my phone bills.

One day he told me about one of his friends, Raju, who was settled in Bhopal. Raju was his class mate and was a South Indian too. Babu Sahab told me his story about how Raju started his own business in Bhopal through hard work and dedication. Today there is a village and township in his name. So it was actually Babu Sahab's wish that I should become like Raju. It was as if Babu Sahab had some intuition that I had the attitude and aptitude to become another Raju. So the God form in his mind was regularly motivating me to start my own business.

To start a business, especially an export business, I needed an office and I started looking for it. As I was jobless at that time, my financial condition did not allow me to take an office on rent. I had a wish to discuss my problem with Babu Sahab. One day I shared this wish with him and he readily agreed to open an office on the ground floor of his house as he had two rooms free in his house and he did not require them even in near future too.

Finally, on the 31st of December 1998, I applied for my export license. I borrowed Rs. 1500 from my girlfriend; who is my wife today and I started my own office in the rooms provided by Babu Sahab on the 1st January 1999. My father was very angry that day but my mother has given me Rs. 500 as her blessing.

So the God form of his mind granted me an office to start my business. My sincere gratitude to Babu Sahab.

Chapter 13

A Bank Manager

We would all like to be considered as good people. The world in which we live today is so chaotic and devoid of human values that one fails to realize the fact that being good to others is the step to achieve success and happiness in life. Realizing your sense of goodness begins with identifying your moral ethics and values.

The second and the most important form of God in person who has helped me selflessly in my next step of business and life is D. Madhusoodanan.

Madhusoodanan, he came in to my life as a stranger, a blessing in disguise. Babu Sahab has been known to me for several years. My father's office was near to Babu Sahab's shop.

Even though, I mentioned Babu Sahab as the first God form in this book, the realization of God form actually started after I met Madhusoodanan. The experience I gained with him was really unbelievable.

My parents were unhappy because I gave up a government job and started a business with nothing in my pocket. They said I was going in the wrong direction and I was being misguided by somebody. We did not have any business person in our family and had no prior experience of business too.

My native place in Kerala is at Varkala and my workplace is in Varanasi (Kashi). Since my father was posted in Varanasi, we were settled here. One day my father told me that a new bank manager from Kerala was coming to Varanasi. Madhu soodanan was the new bank manager.

With the intention of meeting a known South Indian family especially from Kerala, I paid a visit to his place in Varanasi. The first thing which surprised me was that he had been posted as a manager in the Export Section of Canara Bank, Varanasi where I had opened up my account just a couple of days before. He had been transferred to Varanasi from the Varkala Branch which was my native place. What a big coincidence!

He was very happy that I had ventured into a new export business and from that moment onwards, he started motivating me morally. He encouraged me to continue with my export and grow with it. He was the second person who had said with confidence "You can do it." He also said, "The one who lack courage to take action, live a dreary life of mediocrity, agony, frustration and depression. Don't let your regrets and fears overpower your dreams. Have the courage to take control of your life. Have the courage to take charge of your fate and have the courage to take action." Tacking a leaf out of his words, I decided never to look back and with an optimistic attitude, I worked more enthusiastically in my business. In other words, if I say, I am in business I owe it because of not only my confidence but also because of other's confidence in me and the capability that they reposed in me.

From the very first day itself, he started asking me about my day to day actions in running the business. I often discussed with him the problems I faced. At that time, the main medium of communication with international customers was through fax only and Babu Sahab and yet another friend of mine

Rajesh Singh who also ran a PCO helped me to use their fax for my purpose.

One day while talking to Madhusoodanan I came to know that he was unhappy with his transfer to Varanasi as it was very difficult for him to adjust with this city. Apart from that, whenever he left Kerala for Varanasi his son was admitted into the hospital for some health problem. The same thing happened twice and he had to take leave from the bank and go back home for his son's treatment. When he reached home, he recovered very fast and never fell ill after that. But the problem started as soon as he leaves for Varanasi to join his duty.

So the issue of his son and his dislike for the city disturbed him and made him feel very restless and uncomfortable. He started talking to the senior authorities in the bank for his transfer back to Kerala.

Despite his troubles, he supported me morally and kept my morale boosted up. He motivated me day in and day out not to leave my business and continue it in whatever way possible.

One day evening, he called me to his house and asked me to sign on some papers and I did it. The next day evening he visited my home and gave me a cheque of Rs. One Lakh which was in my name. That time it was a huge amount for me and I was afraid of accepting it. I asked him why he had given this amount and that it was a lot of money. I had never seen such a big amount. I was not sure whether I was worthy of taking that amount, and the manner in which I will be able to repay it.

I was hesitant to accept the cheque but he handed over the cheque to me forcibly and told me to use that amount. I can do whatever I want for my business and to grow further. He also said that I should not worry about repaying it, as I had6 to 7 years time to repay. He assured that even if I was not able to repay properly, nobody would arrest me. Truly speaking my hands were shaking while I accepted that cheque. It was as if I had millions in my hand. That day, that amount and those motivational words filled me with confidence.

This was the real the turning point of my life, the most unforgettable day. It was really God in his form who helped me. As I met him just two weeks back as a stranger and he knew nothing about me, I wondered how could he have so much faith in me and my potentials.

A person posted in Canara Bank, Varkala, Kerala transfered to Varanasi and that too in the same section where I had opened my account for business & helping me with such a huge amount…this coincidence enhanced my faith in God. I wonder how God helps those who believe in the beauty of their dreams and helps their dream change into the realm of possibility. Rightly observed Sophocles, a Greek philosopher, "Heaven never helps the person who will not act."

The next day Madhusoodanan accompanied me to buy a computer, printer and helped me to establish dial up internet facility. The very next week I saw an envelope in the post box of my office gate. It was from Japan and it was my first business order worth US $ 3000 on Letter of Credit basis.

Nevertheless to mention, my happiness knew no bounds and tears rolled down my eyes. I handed over the order list to Madhusoodanan. He was thrilled and happy, and congratulated me for my achievement.

But the next problem was how I would arrange the material for export. The order was on Letter of Credit Basis. I had to first ship the material then only I would get the payment.

I needed material worth INR1 Lakh to ship to Japan. How would it happen was a point of concern now.

Chapter 14

A Bead Supplier

Next day a tall person visited my office and introduced him self as Yogendra Singh Yadav, supplier of different kinds of handicraft material to exporters. I was inexperienced and novice in this business, I was also facing financial crunch as it was the most struggling phase of my life. So I did not tell him about the order that I had received because I knew that nobody was going to supply me with material without cash in advance. Even if he had agreed to supply, immediate payment would have proved to be very difficult for me to manage.

But he himself admitted that his purpose for visiting me was that he had heard about my efficiency and attitude from the employees of other companies and he was ready to help me in whatever way, he could. Hearing this, I was bit encouraged and showed him the order I had received. He completely understood the terms and conditions of the order. He said, he will supply me the goods without any advance and I can pay him only after the payment arrives from the customer.

So, it was really the God sent opportunity, one by one in many forms helping me and promoting my business. I was just acting my part in the best way I could.

As promised, he supplied me the goods on time and now I had to pack and ship them.

It was during this time, I came to know that Madhu soodanan will be resigning from his job the next week for good and will be going back to Kerala as it was very difficult for him to manage here.

But it was his wish that before he left the job and went back to Kerala, I should pack the goods and forward the papers through his bank to customer's bank for payment.

Even though, being a Senior Manager of the Bank, he too helped me in packing the goods. We were doing that actually on a Friday night, because the next day Saturday was his last day in the bank and after that he would resign go back to Kerala.

Next day (Saturday) morning I carried the goods to the air agent to ship the goods so that I can provide the post shipment documents to Madhusoodanan through bank to forward them to the customer's bank in Japan for payment. Normally on Saturday the bank works till 12 noon only, but he kept his bank open till 5 pm just for me to forward the papers.

Everything went off successfully and the first export document of my bank through his hand was forwarded to Japan. On Monday he resigned his job and went back to Kerala.

After his transfer from Kerala, he lived in Varanasi for 6 months or so. When I recall those days I feel like his stay in Varanasi was just to promote me in my life and business. It was a blessing in disguise. His real motivation both morally and financially really helped me to grow further in my life. He never visited Varanasi again but he was regularly in touch with me to provide me his valuable advice, motivate me with positivities of life.

Madhusoodanan is an unforgettable God form of my Life. After meeting him, I realized for the first time that I had met God. I pay my sincere gratitude to him.

Yogendra Yadav also continued to support me and once he requested me to help him to start his own export business in his city. He was an MBA but supplied materials to exporters. He did not have the knowhow of starting an export business on his own. Though I am always happy to share whatever knowledge and experience I have with anybody but because of some bitter experiences of the past whilst engaging in such sharing, I rejected his request. However, he requested me to take one more chance on him and wait for 10 years. So I did. Since I had a computer and internet facility, I started getting orders. But it was very difficult to handle some big orders for which huge amounts were needed. Yogendra was financially sound to manage orders of any amount. So what I did was, I visited his city and helped him to start his office and obtain a license etc. Later I passed on all those big orders to him and I continued with small orders which were easily manageable for me. There was no commission or profit sharing between us. The relation was quite transparent.

As per his words, if I check him after 10 years of relation, he made more turnover than me in exports, and he had also diversified his line of business to a higher level. My business and turnover was not even 50% of what his was. But his mentality and attitude remained unchanged. He behaved in the same manner he did when I first met him. Even after 10 years once when I was facing some financial crisis, I never informed him about it. But he could smell it from somebody that I had some problem with finance. He called me up and enquired about it. I told him a little bit about the problem. The next day morning my account was credited with Five lakh Rupees and he didn't stop there. He continued to transfer with many lakhs whenever I required without even thinking whether I would be able to return it to him or not. It means he tried his very best to support me with finance and with moral support too. Till date my relation with him is as smooth & strong as always.

By God's grace, within 5 years, my business had flourished with millions of turnover. I owned multiple vehicles, multiple properties, name fame and enjoyed international travel etc.

A success journey with nothing, even the confidence in me that time was instilledby others; I was motivated by many God forms. It was God's wish to make me prosper. I just realized that God has createda man with immense power and intellect and he could do wonders.

After 10 years of successfully running a business, it started slowing down. Then I planned to enter a new line of business, and at this time when I was in need of financial contribution, no near and dear one supported me.

I agree if our kith and kin do not support us in time of crisis, it is probably because of their lack of confidence in us. However, I proved my capability. Ups and downs, joys and sorrow are part and parcel of one's life. I too had my share. Obviously, at that time I expected help and support from my close relatives. But again, their attitude was same. Even after achieving all this, they did not have the confidence to share their finance with me.

What is the reason of their indifference?

Evidently they still believed that whatever I had gained was a mere farce.

However, I cannot change their mindset. It will remain fixed. They would still derive pleasure in digging up and discussing the regatirities of my life. Time and again they will highlight the innumerable reasons for the downfall of my business and keep advising me everyday instead of lending a helping hand. What they fail to realize is that the experience that I had gained in past so many years will always remain as my asset with me.

Once again Madhusoodanan came to my help. He supported me with seven Lakhs of his own money. It was given to me for a four month period. But my project was delayed for 14 months and his amount was blocked. He was also facing financial crisis during that time, but the surprising thing is that he never pressurized me to send his money back. He understood the situation and empathized with me. This outsider who was neither a blood relation, nor a relative acted as a Love form of God, and that is why he still had the confidence in me, which others did not have.

Noticeably God has his own medium to reach us. It may be through any of his creations, be it some material, animal or man himself.

What intrigued me most was the fact that inspite of being avoided by near and dear ones, what promoted Madhu soodanan to support me? Frankly, he did not expect anything in return from me, because by the grace of God, he is already blessed with wealth and prosperity in abundance.

One more thing I noted in Madhusoodanan that one could discuss any subject with him even though he loved the subject or not. He inter acts taking great interest on the subject and give suitable advice. He will never de-motivates anybody rather discusses the positive and negative aspects of that subject. This quality of his enabled me to sail through smoothly the ups and downs of my business.

I express my sincere gratitude to Madhusoodanan and my friend, Yogendra Singh for becoming the vehicle of God and having appeared as Love form of God in my life.

Chapter 15

An Administration Officer

As I have mentioned earlier, I started my business on1st, January 1999 but the first few months were a period of struggle.

At this stage, the other Love form of God who entered my life was Suresh Nair, who was a railway employee. We know each other because we both belong to Kerala. Incidentally we met in a social gathering at Varanasi and from then on our friendship continued though we have no family connections. My dedication and passion for work enthused him always.

He always told me that I am born to do different things and supported me wherever he could.

One fine morning, in March 1999, on Monday I got a call from him and he asked me to visit his house, but the reason was not mentioned over the phone. Actually he wanted to introduce me to a Project Manager of General Motors Locomotive Division of America who had an office in the Diesel Locomotive Works, Varanasi. I reached his house within an hour. Suresh Nair had called me to offer a job in that company under that Project Manager. But I wondered why he gave me the proposal for that job though two of his own brothers were looking for decent employment. He emphasized that only I was the most suitable person for that job. He wished that I should join the job because of the pressure on him by the Project Manager to introduce an experienced person.

I then, explained him that I was not willing to do any kind of job in the future. I had started my business and I wished to make my own kingdom. I wanted to become a successful entrepreneur and didn't wish to do any kind of job and continue to work as an employee.

Being aware of my financial condition, he pressurized me to join that job and also run my business simultaneously until I became financially sound. He tried to convince me a lot. Just to honour him, I agreed to meet the Project Manager. I thought I would go to meet him and reject the offer.

So he called the Project Manager for an appointment and in half an hour we reached his home instead of his office. He was sitting in the lawn with his wife. The first impression casted helped me guess that he would be a Project Manager of an international company. It was quite obvious through his life style and demeanor.

Suresh Nair introduced me and told him that I had just ventured into a business leaving both private and government jobs and was struggling to establish myself in it. He also assured him that I was capable enough to hand the job efficiently.

After few minutes interaction held at the tea table in the garden itself helped him gauge my potential. He asked me to come to the office after two hours. But I cleared my part and told to the Project Manager that I was disinterested in that job. I put forth my condition that I could give it a try if my independence was not hampered as I needed my freedom and time. He agreed and confirmed that this was a US company where nobody sits on one's head. He said that "you have to finish your responsibilities on time, that's all."

Seeing my financial crisis to establish my business, the God in the form of Suresh Nair came and helped me to join a new type of company where I could work with freedom.

It was only on his insistence that I joined that company. I worked there for seven years whilst doing my own business. It helped me to earn and learn so many things which I shall explain in the next chapter. I express my sincere gratitude to the Love form of God, Suresh Nair.

Chapter 16

India Project Manager - General Motors

Yes, he is the same person, Mr. Suresh Nair had introduced me in the morning. As decided, I reached his office after two hours. He introduced me to the company and explained why they were in an Indian Railway Campus and what they were doing. General Motors will be transferring technology for making a high powered new locomotive in India at the Diesel Locomotive Works, Varanasi.

The work ethics and style of this US Company was poles apart from that of an Indian Company. The first work assigned to me by him was to rearrange some drawings systematically. I did it. The first appreciation I got from him was for my handwriting and the first thing I noticed in him was that he appreciated every endeavor as soon as something good was done by his subordinates.

He held a high grade officer's rank in the company and his salary and facilities were beyond my imagination. He was somber, calm and always had a nice smile on his face. Whoever entered in to the office even if he was a peon or an officer, he welcomed both with same honour and affection; he was such a down to earth and non-egoistical person. Snobbishness never dared to enter his domain of work.

After few days, I realized that I was not working here as an employee, I was here to learn many new things that would open my eyes to see the world in a bigger way, which was much beyond my imagination. The most important thing I learned in my seven years of working with him was his attitude towards work. He always motivated me and I learned this attitude from him to motivate others too. We do not know what capability or efficiency we have within us, but other people like Madhu soodanan, Suresh Nair or Ajay Sinha can feel and understand it well.

He always tried to teach me new things. He helped and advised me on how to make progress in my business too. He also shared many of his experiences of life with me. But he never asked me to give up my business because I was doing a job there; rather he also enjoyed and appreciated the growth of my business.

I was not doing a job there actually I was learning many new things which I could not have learnt from any school or college, I learnt to understand people, understand their attitude and understand the world. There was a big difference in the attitude and mentality of Indian Employees working for the Indian Railways and the attitude of US employees. There I could interact with many US Engineers who visited here as a part of the technology transfer. I used to watch and learn from Ajay Sinha, how he managed even in critical situations there without getting anxious or angry.

After a few months of my working there, he started delegating new responsibilities on my shoulder. I also got involved in the working style of that office and used to spend more than eight hours a day there because it was not a working place for me, rather it was a learning place and I enjoyed every moment I spent there. The amount of remuneration I was getting there was also five times more than that of any other Indian company. So no doubt, to run my little export company, my job really helped and I was also educated in so many new things which I could have experienced or learnt from formal schooling. Today everybody is impressed with my attitude but it was really a gift from Ajay Sinha who encouraged me at every gate of my life and help me stand up renewed energy and vivaciousness. He also used to do a lot of Tithing. I remember one of my customers, Michelle Hayes from Syracuse, New York who said to me "You have that attitude and aptitude that built America," which was a very big compliment.

After a few years working there, Mr Sinha had to undergo bypass surgery all of a sudden. It was a difficult time for the office. His presence was very necessary because he had to complete a particular project in that month and only after that General Motors would be getting a payment (in millions) from India Railways as per their contract. But everybody in the company was anxious because of his health. At that time the Indian Head of the company was Mr. Pesi Vazifdar at New Delhi. Due to Ajay Sinha's appreciation and compliments, I enjoyed a good reputation in the company.

Pesi Vazifdar – I have no words to describe about him, I had never met such a cool personality in my life. I learned a lot from his attitude too.

Pesi Vazifdar called me and asked me how to manage the situation because it would take months' for Ajay to resume his work. But I asked Pesi to allow me to continue with that particular work in the office and I would try my best to get it done before the due date so that the company is not in hot waters.

The actual work that I had to do was to show Indian Railways that all the required drawings had been received properly and had been systematically entered into their record.

I had to convince the top officers of the Railways and to get certificates from all of them. For this I had to get in touch with an Indian Railway's staff, Mr. Malviyaji who was an aged person. In our office most of the work, was to managed on Microsoft Excel, but I had never learnt it formally. Whatever expertise I had gained in Microsoft Office was only while synchronizing the drawings. This responsibility was again like a boon from God to learn and experience new things.

Mr. Malviya helped me a lot in learning Microsoft Excel. Till date whenever I open the 'wrap text' option under Text Control of Format Alignment I remember him. There was one more officer at that time at General Motors Delhi Office, Pankaj Sachdeva who taught me a lot of mathematical formulas in Excel over the phone. He never hesitated to teach me anything. Whenever Ajay asked him to do some work in Excel in Delhi, he called me and gave that work to me to do it myself under his guidance. I always accepted it with pleasure because I knew that I was going to learn something from it.

In this way, the Love form of God in Pankaj Sachdeva and Mr. Malviya helped me to learn unlimited things on Microsoft Office. Unfortunately, Pankay Sachdeva left the company and joined another company but till date at-least once or twice a year we speak over the phone wherever we are.

Finally I was able to complete the job within the stipulated timeline. I convinced the railway officers, obtained the certificate and the fund was transferred to General Motors on time. By that time, Ajay had also rejoined the company. Contrary to my expectations, he did not appreciate me as I had expected. I thought probably his ego had crashed upon him that a small employee of yesteryears, had handled such a big job efficiently which he could only handle. But I was under a wrong impression. After a few days, one day in the morning Ajay told me that Pesi Vazifdar is coming to Varanasi just to meet me. Confused, I thought, "Why Pesi is coming to meet me? Who am I? I guess he is going to appoint me as a permanent employee in the company, but that I would not agree to because I wanted to do my own business, I could not give up and compromise for a permanent job in this company"

So I was quite ready to reject that offer if it came, but all my thoughts and ideas were wrong.

He came with a nice greeting card and a letter of appreciation. "Superb Jagadeesh! We all proud of you and appreciate your efforts. Wonderful." This was written on the card. My eyes were filled with tears. He also gave me a Cheque of Rs. 10,000 as a reward on behalf of the company for accepting the challenge and getting it executed. It was Ajay behind the entire scene who planned to silently appreciate me with such a big surprise.

I gave that amount back to him towards my contribution to the collection they were doing to help people in Gujarat who were affected by an Earthquake. His appreciation was enough to satisfy me rather I was happy and thankful to God that I was able to successfully accept and complete that challenge.

For seven years, I worked there and when I became busy in my business with month's long international visits and other engagements. I left that job. But those seven years were like God had put me in a college to learn many small and big things from there. Ajay Sinha shifted to Delhi long back and he was promoted to higher ranks also. But even to this day at-least once in a month he calls me and enquires about my well being. His motivation has encouraged me to get the most out of my life. After Ajay shifted to Delhi, Mr. Vishwas Moktali after resigning his railway job joined as a new Project Manager of the company. Again words are not enough to detail the fantastic attitude of Vishwas. He never behaved like a boss instead like a brother who cares.

My sincere gratitude is due to Ajay Sinha, Pesi Vazifdar, Pankaj Sachdeva, Vishwas Moktali, Natarajan Rethinam and Malviyaji for being there with the Love form of God to help me cherish and savour those unforgettable moments etched well down in the memory lane of my life, thereby leaving an indelible mark on my slate.

Chapter 17

Abu Dhabi Connection

Another strange way of realizing the Love form of God is through Somettan, one of the great persons I ever met in my life.

The actual meeting with this person, its purpose and the end result were all strange and I had different experience altogether. We wonder how the 'Love form of God' works for us and in what ways. We cannot even imagine the climax of the story that was created by God.

I am a die-hard fan of the famous South Indian singer Yesudas. His devotional songs are very popular in the South. I wished to write some devotional songs for him and I did it. After composing the lyrics, I searched on the internet how I could send it to him because he is a celebrity and he is beyond my reach. It is not easy to meet him either. There was a forum on the net to discuss about the singer Yesudas. So I also posted my wish to send my devotional lyrics to Yesudas. The next day I received an email asking me to send the lyrics. It was Somettan and he wrote to me from Abu Dhabi. I emailed them to him. After reading it, he appreciated advised me to send them to Vinod Yesudas, the son of Yesudas. He also provided me with his mail id. As advised by Vinod Yesudas, I completed the formality and sent the lyrics to him by courier. During that day I got a chance to speak to the famous singer Yesudas over the phone too.

But my relation with Somettan continued. Every day we were in touch with each other through exchange of mails. After a few months, one day he asked me to help him with an archaeology book for his daughter. He tried his best to find it all over India but in vain. He shared his problem with me. I also tried at so many places in India but I couldn't arrange it. I started searching it internationally through my business clients. After a lot of searching an Australian buyer found it in a library of her city. In reciprocation, I offered extra materials to her in my next shipment against that book. She arranged and couriered the book to me. In that way I could help Somettan with that book. Obviously they were very happy and later I came to know that in the final examination his daughter, Nimi, bagged Gold Medal in her college. They invited me to attend the function in the college, unfortunately, I could not make it because of my busy schedule at that time.

During that period, my brother-in-law in Kerala was trying to get a job in the UAE. It was his dream to get a job there and for that he had been trying for years and years. He was now at a stage where he was about to give up.

So I invited him to Varanasi to engage him in my line of business. But his mind was set for a job in the UAE only. So I thought to give it a try. Then one day, I shared this matter with Somettan. I thought probably I will lose him if I disturb him with such demands. But he took up this matter seriously and requested me to send him through a visiting visa with an arrangement for his stay there for two months. For this one of my friends, Mehtab who was also working in Abu Dhabi helped me in arranging a visiting visa for him and that way my brother–in-law flew to Abu Dhabi. His accommodation and visiting visa was provided by Mehtab and his brother-in-law who had lived there for many years. Somettan sent him every day to new companies for interviews. He strictly said that my brother-in-law must be well experienced to get the job, otherwise he will have to come back. But my brother-in-law was over confident of his efficiency. Unfortunately he could not pass the interview anywhere. So Somettan was little annoyed with me for sending him without rich experience in his field. Later I asked my brother in law, what should be done. He said that he will return to India as his experience was not enough to get a job there.

I requested Somettan to adjust him somewhere at least as a trainee so that he could build-up his life and gain some experience. The Love form of God within Somettan heard my request and he adjusted him in a company as a trainee. Now for the last few years he has been working there successfully and has established himself well.

Actually the relation started with Somettan through devotional lyrics but the meeting was to fulfill different purposes for mutual benefit. Here the gainer was my brother in law. But ultimately it was my win. When all others failed to offer him a job in the UAE, even his uncles who had been working there for 25 years, neglected him, I took the challenge to help him from here.

When I accepted that challenge, the God sent a person in the form of Somettan and the Love form of God within him helped me to fulfill my promise.

We are still in contact and we also share our family matters too. I was there to attend his daughter's marriage in Kerala. Once when I visited Dubai, Somettan came to meet me from Abu Dhabi in his car driving for more than two hours. That was the depth of our relation that God had created between us. Sometimes these relationships are more deeper and thicker than blood relations.

I wish to express my sincere gratitude to Somettan for being there with his continued blessings.

Chapter 18

Two Media Friends

Padma Kumar is a professional gazal singer and Vipin Chandran is a professional camera man.

A question that has intrigued me most is what form of love might have worked through these two persons? They have not added any wealth or prosperity in my life. Here the Love form of God worked to help me broaden my horizons and find and leverage my hidden potential.

They both used to visit Varanasi for gazal programmes and for making films. As I mentioned earlier, I am a fan of Yesudas and I used sing and practice his spiritual songs especially in Malayalam language. Padmakumar is from Kerala. He sings both Hindi and Urdu Gazals. He cannot converse in Hindi, however, his singing in Hindi is par excellence.

As I was well settled in my business, I used to often call him giving him offers to hold gazal programmes in the city and this was a part and parcel of my life. It gave me immense pleasure and a sense of enjoyment and fulfillment as well. Before meeting Padmakumar, I was a blind follower of Yesudas only. He used to teach me various methods of singing and especially changed my mind from my addiction to Malayalam songs to Urdu and Hindi gazal singing. He never taught me music, but taught me the tactics and nuances of vocal singing technique; that is how to add emotions and feelings; how to pronounce certain words, in order to lay emphasis on them so that the feeling of a song could touch the heart of the audience while singing. I gradually changed my singing attitude to a different level and then I started singing many Hindi and Urdu gazals too. Today I enjoy listening and singing gazals to my level of satisfaction.

So the Love form of God within Padmakumar helped me to understand music on a different plane.

Vipin Chandran, his friend is a camera man who films for his music albums. Vipin is a gold medalist and has expertise in his field.

I must acknowledge that since the time I met Vipin Chandran and Padmakumar, I have found a drastic change in my attitude towards singing, listening to music and friends. Initially, I had no intention of joining media because it never lured me. But with the entry of Padmakumar and Vipin Chandran in my life, I was able to discover my hidden talents and this has always paid me dividence. Thus, I owe a lot to my friends.

Apart from singing, Padmakumar is also a good cameraman and editor too. So Vipin and Padmakumar while shooting used to teach me the techniques of using a camera. They have taught me many things and I grasped many things while watching them filming. Padmakumar has also set up a small studio in my house where he edit his videos. Sometimes when he was bored of editing, he asked me to help. Having an innate inquisitiveness to explore new arenas, I always tried my best to help him whenever I got a chance to edit or use a camera. Later, Vipin helped me to have an editing machine and he taught me how to use a camera, over the phone. Now I have also started making my own albums and documentaries. If I need to learn more techniques, I google and learn through youtube tutorials to enhance my knowledge.

In the year 2013, I won a place in the Guinness Book of World Records for making an animation film in the shortest time. God has sent two people into my life in the form of Padmakumar and Vipin Chandran. Their Love form of God helped me and that's why I am able to do so many things in the media. I have won many accolades and awards in that field too. I extend my sincere gratitude to Padmakumar and Vipin Chandran for being there to help me flourish in my life.

Chapter 19

A Teacher who Walks beside Me

While I was searching for a right person to guide me by googling I came across with the name of Dr. Subramonian as a Guinness Book of World Record Holder in Teachiing. OMG, even God has also changed his ways of communication. God showed light unto so many people around me but he has chosen only a few of them for me to act though as a tool to help me to grow further in various fields.

He was my guide and supporter to doctorate in Humanities. He also helped me in organizing the Guinness attempt. I had actually approached him for a Guinness Record attempt on a different subject, but assessing my ability and talent in film making and other multi-tasking ability on the computer he advised me to attempt for making an animation film within the shortest possible time. He said that the existing record holder at that time in this subject was a Canadian, who had done it in six hours and if I try it, I can break it. He trained me for six months and with the passage of time, I learnt how to achieve it within the time frame. He used to tell me only constant effort and belief in the supreme will take a person to achievements of any level. He did the whole liasoning with the Guinness Book of World Records authorities in London on my behalf. God used Dr. Subramonian as a tool for my achievement as God himself is the ultimate form of love. With his well wishes and training, I was able to break the record by making an animation film in three and a half hours and now I am proud that the record is held even today in the name of our mother country. Dr. Subramonian helped me to get two titles in my career one as Doctorate and another as a Guinness Book of World Record.

I would like to narrate one incident which made me write this book at one time when I met him, he was very busy with the authoring of his book "Professor's Diary" An amazing first person narrative of one man's journey through life...

Starting out as a very ordinary child, full of childish pranks, and an average student, who is not above playing truant from classes, or skipping studies till just before the exams, this is the story of the author's gradual growth into a rank-winner, an esteemed teacher, and a much regarded Professor and Principal, who goes on to win several national and international awards and recognitions.

Throughout the story, his commitment to truth and ethical standards, and his faith in his students and the genuine desire for their well –being stands out...

Unconditional faith in the Supreme, and a deep vein of spirituality, sustain him in times of crises, and he comes out of many trials unscathed.

The style of his writing influenced me a lot and I have got no other way to imitate him and it is said "imitation is the best form of appreciation."

Apart from this, even today he is in constant touch with me and is continuously motivating me to discover new unexplored areas in the human life as a friend who is walking along with me.

Chapter 20

A Businessman Cum Politician

Mr. Ramakrishna Iyyangar is a renowned businessman and a politician. His role was to re-build the collapsed career of my life. After running my business successfully for many years, a jolt was given by China when they duplicated our export product. Consequently, we had to shut down our business and suffer a period of inactivity. Life was again a struggle. The business was not shut down in one day, but gradually. By that time we realized that it was because of China's duplication of our product, the company started incurring a loss. Later we had to temporarily close it. But the life style and operational expenses were just the same. The employees were being accommodated for years till the time the income stopped completely. Then I had to terminate them one by one though with a heavy heart. At the same time I learnt to control my expenses and life style. I had many other fields to earn money, but for the last few years, life became very hard as flow of finance was heavily disrupted. I cannot explain the phase that I had been through but it was far and worse than I had ever expected. Since I did not have any bad habit, and I was surrounded with many great people in the Love form of God, I survived in whatever way possible. Probably it was another training period of God to make me more mature to handle the future success in my career ahead. So the days passed by but I kept on trying to learn new things and spent time for good purposes. Many a times I became disheartened, but in some way, through somebody or even through a book I was reading, I kept up my enthusiasm and was able to gain new experiences. During this period I had been given a chance to understand my near and dear ones. Who came to render help and who did not help. I understood, who was jealous of my success and who would exploit me in my bad time. Yet the Love form of God helped me to survive whilst opening new doors and opportunities to brave the world.

Actually my guess was right! God was making me more mature during these years to manage a big success in my career ahead. I had never ever associated myself with politics as I had no interest in it. Once when I visited one of my friend's house, some election campaign meeting was going on, I saw that Ramakrishna Iyyangar was delivering an impressive speech which catered every ones attention. So I met him there. From the next day onwards, I also joined him to attend the meetings and he also very quickly adopted me as usual like others had done and the relation grew up and we soon became like brothers. I was impressed with his attitude and he was impressed with my attitude. Anyway I smelt that the Love form of God within him has something to do for me. The relation continued. The election was over and his party won and came to power. I realized that he was not in politics for making name and power, rather it was to work for the nation. After a month whilst talking with him he asked if he could help me in any way. I explained what I was facing in my career now. I had a project in mind which I thought would be beneficial for the country. I showed it to him and he was impressed with it and promised me that such kinds of projects are very necessary for the country and he would surely help to get it expedited. With this particular project, my career would take a new turn which would be ten times better than earlier. This time I understood that it was very necessary to pass some difficult situation in life to give a break from the past and to prepare afresh for a new venture.

I thank the Love form of God within Ramakrishna Iyyangar and for being there to provide support for my life ahead.

Chapter 21

Two Authors

I once again admit profusely that the Love form of God had to play an imperative role for me to write further and to complete this book. I owe my allegiance to God to help me complete it.

While surfing the net I bought some books of Sri Vishwanath through Amazon. He is one of the Amazon's best selling author. As I am an avid reader, I ordered four of his books online. While reading one of his books "SHIVA," I felt as if each and every sentence of the book was like a communication between God and me. God was making me understand how to realize the power of self. God was telling me, who I am and what immense capacity I was holding and what great thing still I could do. I am more precious and hard than diamond. Nobody can steal my shine, charm and importance.

All the words in his book were like the Love form of God and God's conversation and advices to me. The author Sri Vishwanath, created some fiction wisely to understand the true form of us and the true form of God. Even though, I had good thoughts and experience about God, his one sentence touched me very much. "The Creator is great, not the creation." We usually worry about the creation, but when we have constant understanding and faith in the Creator, nothing will affect us.

So after reading four of his books, I was reenergized and rejuvenated. The next day I sent him an email thanking him for writing such great books and my reviews about them. He immediately acknowledged my mail just as he acknowledged all of his readers. The next day in the afternoon, he called me up from the US and talked to me for at-least half an hour. It was the beginning of a new Love form of God's interaction with me. He was unknown to me until I bought his book. Having no knowledge about my motive of life, he started motivating me with many good words and his experiences. I wondered why he was motivating me, and why he was sharing all his experiences with me without me. I assume it was God's plan and the Love form of God within him that was working for me.

I also told him about my plan to write a book in future which would be titled **"The Moments When I Met God."** He was overwhelmed and said that the title was very impressive. From the next day he started mailing me his sincere advices and motivated me to write the book as soon as possible.

The day when I received the first call from Sri Vishwanath, I got another call from a nearby temple requesting me to visit there to meet somebody. I reached there in half an hour. It was Mr. Sadanandan Pillai, famous write from South India. He was writing books on temples all over India and he needed my help to see the temples of Varanasi.

It was just a coincidence that I met two authors one over the phone and the other in person. Mr Sadanandan Pillai was a retired principal of a school and he presented me with one of his latest books of more than 1200 pages. He encouraged me to continue my writing and assured that he would extend his help in the best manner possible. Excitedly in the evening,

I looked for my note book in the almirah which I had kept somewhere seven years ago. As it was pre-planned by God, I found it within five minutes.

So the Love form of God and His God force in the form of Sri Vishwanath and Sadanandan Pillai created an impact on me and I restarted my writing of this book. Surprisingly the energy from God forced me to complete the later half of this book within seven days after a gap of seven years.

I would like to express my sincere gratitude to two great authors Sri Vishwanath and Sadanandan Pillai.

The success of this book has to go a long way because this book is not written by me, but created by God's will to motivate millions around the world to understand the Love form of God, the real God.

Last but the least

My sincere gratitude to the Lord of Universe for making this dream come true.

It's my duty to express my gratitude by sharing my experiences with the new generation.

Anybody can mail me if he has any doubt in life or is struggling with problems in attaining success.

I will be happy to share my experience and advice within the bounds of my knowledge.

Just send an email to

iwillcareu@gmail.com